Practical Liturgies for the School Year

Sr. Mary Fearon, RSM

BROWN-ROA

A Division of Harcourt Brace & Company

Dubuque, Iowa

Bible Excerpts

The New American Bible, copyright © 1970 by The Confraternity of Christian Doctrine, Washington, D.C.

The New American Bible with Revised New Testament, copyright © 1986 by The Confraternity of Christian Doctrine, Washington, D.C.

The Jerusalem Bible. Copyright © 1966 by Darton, Longman & Todd, Ltd. and Doubleday & Company, Inc.

Book Team

Publisher—Ernest T. Nedder
Editorial Director—Sandra Hirstein
Production Manager—Marilyn Rothenberger
Art Director—Cathy Frantz

ISBN 0–697–02999–9

10 9 8

Contents

Opening Mass Celebration for Faculty

Theme: We come to celebrate the beginning of our school year.

Entrance Procession: Traditional

Gathering Song: "Come with Me Into the Fields," Dan Schutte, *Glory & Praise* 1

First Reading: Deuteronomy 7:6–11

Second Reading: Psalm 139:1–7, 9–14 (Choral Reading)

Alleluia: Chorus of "Thank You, Lord," Carey Landry, *Hi God!*

Gospel: John 15:15–17

Homily: Comments on Gospel and a welcome to new beginnings

General Intercessions: Prayed by teachers from each grade level

Preparation Hymn: "Here I Am, Lord," Dan Schutte, *Glory & Praise* 3

Gifts Procession: Teachers bring up gifts of bread and wine.

Holy, Holy, Holy: "Holy, Holy, Holy," Bob Dufford and Dan Schutte, *Glory & Praise* 1

Memorial Acclamation: "Christ Has Died . . ." Missalette

Amen: "Lilies of the Field," *Reader's Digest*

The Lord's Prayer: Missalette (Choose one familiar to parish)

Lamb of God: Missalette (Choose one familiar to parish)

Communion Hymn: "Sing a New Song," Dan Schutte, *Glory & Praise* 1

Communal Prayer of Thanksgiving: *Prayers for the Domestic Church,* Edward Hays (Easton, KS: Forest of Peace Books, 1977), page 47

Recessional Hymn: "City of God," Dan Schutte, *Glory & Praise* 3, verses 1 and 2, and refrain

Opening Mass Celebration for Faculty

Theme

Leader: Today, we come together to celebrate the opening of a new school year. When books, or packages, are opened, something is revealed. If we never open them, we never experience the revelation. Let us ask God to help us have the courage to open our year with a spirit of joy and expectation and to receive gratefully the gift that the year brings. We pray that we be open to our mission to (school or parish) faculty, parents, and children.

BROWN-ROA, a division of Harcourt Brace & Company

Opening Mass Celebration for Faculty

Reading I:

Deuteronomy 7:6–11

God's election and favour

If Yahweh set his heart on you and chose you, it was not because you outnumbered other peoples; you were the least of all peoples. It was for love of you and to keep the oath he swore to your fathers that Yahweh brought you out with his mighty hand and redeemed you from the house of slavery, from the power of Pharaoh king of Egypt. Know then that Yahweh your God is God indeed, the faithful God who is true to his covenant and his graciousness for a thousand generations towards those who love him and keep his commandments, but who punishes in their own persons those that hate him. He is not slow to destroy the man who hates him; he makes him work out his punishment in person. You are therefore to keep and observe the commandments and statutes and ordinances that I lay down for you today.

BROWN-ROA, a division of Harcourt Brace & Company

Opening Mass Celebration for Faculty

Reading II:

Psalm 139:1–7, 9–14

(two teachers)

First Reader:
Yahweh, you examine me and know me. You know if I am standing or sitting. You read my thoughts from far away.

Second Reader:
Whether I walk or lie down, you are watching. You know every detail of my conduct.

First Reader:
The word is not even on my tongue, Yahweh, before you know all about it. Close behind and close in front you fence me round, shielding me with your hand.

Second Reader:
Your knowledge is beyond my understanding, a height to which my mind cannot attain. Where could I go to escape your spirit? Where could I flee from your presence?

First Reader:
If I flew to the point of sunrise, or westward across the sea, your hand would still be guiding me, your right hand holding me.

Second Reader:
If I asked darkness to cover me, and light to become night around me, that darkness would not be dark to you, night would be as light as day.

First Reader:
It was you who created my inmost self, and put me together in my mother's womb.

Second Reader:
For all these mysteries I thank you: for the wonder of myself, for the wonder of your works.

BROWN-ROA, a division of Harcourt Brace & Company

Opening Mass Celebration for Faculty

General Intercessions:

Please respond, "Lord, hear our prayer."

1. For the talents of our Church leaders, teachers, and all in leadership positions, let us pray to the Lord.

All: Lord, hear our prayer.

2. For peace and understanding in our world, let us pray to the Lord.

All: Lord, hear our prayer.

3. For all new teachers, families, and students in our school and parish, let us pray to the Lord.

All: Lord, hear our prayer.

4. For a new year to celebrate our gifts together by working, praying, and caring for one another, let us pray to the Lord.

All: Lord, hear our prayer.

5. For God's blessing on each of us, we pray to God our loving Father.

All: Lord, hear our prayer.

BROWN-ROA, a division of Harcourt Brace & Company

Opening Mass Celebration for Faculty

Prayer after Communion:

*Teachers, Grades 1–7
(Include new teachers
if possible.)*

1. Blessed are you, Lord our God, who has given to each of us a personal destiny and purpose in life.

2. We thank You, God of mysterious ways, that You have a holy design for each of us.

3. We rejoice that each of us is special to You, that our names are written in the palm of Your hand and that our place in history, our purpose for existing, is known within Your heart since endless ages.

4. We are grateful for that long line of holy people who, since ancient times, have inspired others by their faithfulness to their own special destinies.

5. They, by their very lives, shout out to us not to compromise our destinies, not to spoil Your eternal design.

6. Blessed are You, for teachers, parents, and other guides who call us out from the cocoon of comfort and contentment to embark on that unique path which You have set forth for each of Your sons and daughters.

7. Blessed are You, Lord our God, who have given to each of us a personal destiny and purpose in life.

Amen.

Prayers for the Domestic Church, page 47.

BROWN-ROA, a division of Harcourt Brace & Company

Opening Mass Celebration for Students

Theme: We come to celebrate the beginning of a new school year. We bring our special talents and share them with one another. (Introduction by principal.)

Entrance Procession: Cross bearer, servers, Eucharistic ministers, lector, priest celebrant

Gathering Song: "Play Before the Lord," Bob Dufford, *Glory & Praise* 1

First Reading: Ecclesiastes 3:1–9 (teacher)

Responsorial Psalm: "Peace Is Flowing Like a River," Carey Landry. *Glory & Praise* 1, refrain

Second Reading: 1 Corinthians 1:4–7 (student)

Gospel Acclamation: The antiphon of "Glory and Praise to Our God," Dan Schutte, *Glory & Praise* 1

Gospel: Matthew 25:14–30 (celebrant and four students)

Homily: Welcome to a new school where we, as a community, share one another's talents and gifts.

General Intercessions: Petitions prayed by students (grades one through eight)

Preparation Hymn: "Here I Am, Lord," Dan Schutte, *Glory & Praise* 3, (first verse and refrain)

Gifts Procession: Two children carry bread and wine.

Holy, Holy, Holy: "Holy," Bob Dufford and Dan Schutte, *Glory & Praise* 1

Memorial Acclamation: "Christ Has Died . . ." music by Tim Schoenbachler, *Glory & Praise* 1

Amen: "Lilies of the Field," *Reader's Digest*

The Lord's Prayer: Recite

Lamb of God: Recite

Communion Hymn: "One Bread, One Body," John Foley, *Glory & Praise* 1

Communal Prayer of Thanksgiving: "The Prayer of St. Francis" (student from eighth grade)

Recessional Hymn: "Rejoice in the Lord Always," Carey Landry, *Hi God!*

Opening Mass Celebration for Students

Introduction:

(Principal)

Welcome back to _____ School. Today, we are brought together to celebrate the opening of a new school year. Let us ask God to help us have the courage to open our year with a spirit of joy and expectation. Let us receive gratefully the gifts that the year brings. We pray that we become a family of God, sharing and loving one another. Let us stand and welcome our celebrant in song.

BROWN-ROA, a division of Harcourt Brace & Company

Opening Mass Celebration for Students

Readings

First Reading: Ecclesiastes 3:1–9	The first reading is from Ecclesiastes.
	There is a season for everything, a time for every occupation under heaven:
Teacher:	A time for giving birth, a time for dying; a time for planting, a time for uprooting what has been planted.

The first reading is from Ecclesiastes.

There is a season for everything, a time for every occupation under heaven:

A time for giving birth,
a time for dying;
a time for planting,
a time for uprooting what has been planted.

A time for killing,
a time for healing;
a time for knocking down,
a time for building.

A time for tears,
a time for laughter;
a time for mourning,
a time for dancing.

A time for throwing stones away,
a time for gathering them up;
a time for embracing,
a time to refrain from embracing.

A time for searching,
a time for losing;
a time for keeping,
a time for throwing away.

A time for tearing,
a time for sewing;
a time for keeping silent,
a time for speaking.

A time for loving,
a time for hating;
a time for war,
a time for peace.

BROWN-ROA, a division of Harcourt Brace & Company

This is the Word of the Lord.

All:

Thanks be to God.

Second Reading:
1 Corinthians 1:4–7

The second reading is from Paul's letter to the Corinthians.

Student:

I continually thank my God for you because of the favor he has bestowed on you in Christ Jesus, in whom you have been richly endowed with every gift of speech and knowledge.

Likewise, the witness I bore to Christ has been confirmed among you that you lack no spiritual gift as you wait for the revelation of our Lord Jesus Christ.

He will strengthen you to the end, so that you will be blameless on the day of our Lord Jesus [Christ]. God is faithful, and it was he who called you to fellowship with his Son, Jesus Christ our Lord.

This is the Word of the Lord.

All:

Thanks be to God.

BROWN-ROA, a division of Harcourt Brace & Company

Opening Mass Celebration for Students

Gospel (See Matthew 25:14–30)

Each of us has talents and gifts. Sometimes we hide them like the foolish servant in a parable Jesus once told.

Reader:
A man who was going abroad summoned his servants and entrusted his money to them, each according to his ability.

Master:
(to the first man) I will give you five talents; (to the second man) I will give you two talents; (to the third man) I will give you one talent.

Reader:
Then the master set out.

First man:
I will trade my five talents for five more.

Second man:
I will trade my two talents for two more.

Third man:
I will dig a hole and hide my one talent. It will be safe until my master returns.

Reader:
When the master of those servants came back, he went through his accounts with the three men.

First man:
You gave me five talents, sir. Here are five more I have made.

Master:
Well done, good and faithful servant.

Second man:
Sir, you gave me two talents; I invested them wisely and I give you back four talents.

BROWN-ROA, a division of Harcourt Brace & Company

Master:

Well done, good and faithful servant. You both have shown me you can be faithful in small things. I will trust you with greater. Come and join in your master's happiness.

Third man:

Sir, because I know you are a hard man, and because I was afraid, I hid the talent that you gave me. Here it is; it is yours. You can have it back.

Master:

You wicked, lazy servant! Why didn't you at least deposit my money with the bank? On return, I could have recovered my money with interest. I am going to take your one talent and give it to the man who has five talents. To the person who has something, more will be given. To the one who does nothing with what he has, even what he has will be taken away.

BROWN-ROA, a division of Harcourt Brace & Company

Opening Mass Celebration for Students

General Intercessions

A child from each grade comes forward.

The response to each petition is, "Lord, hear our prayer."

Eighth Grader:
For all new students, teachers, and their families whom we welcome to our school, we pray to the Lord.

All: Lord, hear our prayer.

Seventh Grader:
In thanksgiving for a new year to celebrate our gifts together by working, praying, and caring for one another, we pray to the Lord.

All: Lord, hear our prayer.

Sixth Grader:
In thanksgiving for the talents of our Church leaders, teachers, and all who guide us, we pray to the Lord.

All: Lord, hear our prayer.

Fifth Grader:
For our parents who care and love us, we pray to the Lord.

All: Lord, hear our prayer.

Fourth Grader:
For children who are poor and hungry, we pray to the Lord.

All: Lord, hear our prayer.

Third Grader:
In thanksgiving for rainbows, and butterflies, for blue skies, and autumn colors, we pray to the Lord.

All: Lord, hear our prayer.

BROWN-ROA, a division of Harcourt Brace & Company

Second Grader:
In thanksgiving for God who is our loving Father, we pray to the Lord.

All: Lord, hear our prayer.

First Grader:
For our country, we pray to the Lord.

All: Lord, hear our prayer.

BROWN-ROA, a division of Harcourt Brace & Company

Opening Mass Celebration for Students

Communal Thanksgiving:

"The Prayer of St. Francis"

Eighth Grader

Lord, make me an instrument of Your peace;

Where there is hatred, let me sow love;

Where there is doubt, faith;

Where there is despair, hope;

Where there is darkness, light;

And where there is sadness, joy.

O Divine Master,

Grant that I may not so much seek to be consoled,

as to console;

To be understood, as to understand;

To be loved, as to love;

For it is in giving that we receive;

It is in pardoning that we are pardoned;

And it is in dying that we are born to eternal life.

BROWN-ROA, a division of Harcourt Brace & Company

Halloween Celebration: Eve of All Saints

Theme:	We come together to celebrate All Hallows' Eve, better known as Halloween. We are called to celebrate **our** call to holiness.
Entrance Procession:	Traditional, with representative from each class carrying saint poster
Penitential Rite:	"Lord have mercy . . ."
Gloria:	Recited
Opening Prayer:	Celebrant
First Reading:	Philippians 4:4–10 (student)
Responsorial Psalm:	"Glory and Praise to Our God," Dan Schutte, *Glory & Praise* 1
Alleluia:	Cantor, and response by all
Gospel:	John 6:1–13
Homily:	Our call to holiness (and speak to the traditional custom of wearing masks)
Creed:	Missalette (all)
General Intercessions:	Prayed by students, grades one through eight
Preparation Hymn:	"Hail Mary: Gentle Woman," Carey Landry, *Glory & Praise* 1
Gifts Procession:	Two children carry bread and wine (grade five).
Eucharistic Prayer:	Children's Lectionary No. 3
Holy, Holy, Holy:	"Holy," Bob Dufford and Dan Schutte, *Glory & Praise* 1 (sung)
The Lord's Prayer:	Recited while participants hold hands
Sign of Peace:	Handshake
Lamb of God:	Recite
Communion Hymn:	"Blest Be the Lord," Dan Schutte, *Glory & Praise* 1
Communal Prayer of Thanksgiving:	Echo Prayer is led by commentator with gestures.
Recessional Song:	"When the Saints Go Marching In," *Reader's Digest, Focus on Music*

Preparation:

Each class chooses a class saint. Then, before the Mass celebration, the class designs a banner or poster depicting qualities found in that saint, for example, St. Catherine of Siena—courage, faith, love, justice, hope, peace, prayerfulness. At the Mass, Class representatives, carrying the posters or banners, will process in with the celebrants. Also before the Mass, each child designs his/her own Saint Name Tag to wear for the service. The Eucharistic minister will call each child by his/her saint name as the child receives the Lord in communion.

Afterwards, the child places his/her own Saint Name Tag in room at home to remember to pray to the saint for intercession. The children find out about their saints and why their parents gave them that saint's name.

Eve of All Saints

BROWN-ROA, a division of Harcourt Brace & Company

Mass Commentator:

Today we come together in joy. Gathered around the Lord's table, we know that we are members of one family. We are called by name to follow Jesus. We are called to be saints. God is our Father, Jesus is our Brother, the Holy Spirit lives in our hears. Let us sing out with joy as God's Holy Family to greet our celebrant, _____.

(priest)

Celebrant:

Our baptism is a sign that we are members of one family, the Church. As members of God's family, we gather together around the Lord's Table to celebrate Eucharist and to share the one food God gives us all, Jesus. Let us ask forgiveness for the times when we have not lived as one family.

Jesus asks us to live as members of one family. We must try to do so even when it is hard. For the times we acted as if we were better than others, let us pray, "Lord, have mercy."

All: Lord, have mercy.

Celebrant:

For the times we have made fun of others or said unkind things about them, let us say, "Christ, have mercy."

All: Christ, have mercy.

Celebrant:

For the times we were mean to those who love us most, let us say, "Lord, have mercy."

All: Lord, have mercy.

All: The Gloria.

Celebrant:

(Opening Prayer) God, our Father, we became a member of our family by our birth; we became a member of Your family, the Church, by our baptism. Help us to always try to live as one family, to reach out to one another in love, and to care for each other as You care for us. We ask this in the name of Jesus, who gives us Himself as our Food.

All: Amen.

Let us pause and welcome God's Word as He speaks to us in Scripture.

Eve of All Saints

First Reading:

Philippians 4:4–10

Rejoice in the Lord always!
I say it again. Rejoice!

Everyone should see how unselfish you are.
The Lord is near.

Dismiss all anxiety from your minds. Present your needs to God in every form of prayer and in petitions full of gratitude.

Then God's own peace, which is beyond all understanding, will stand guard over your hearts and minds, in Christ Jesus.

Finally, my brothers and sisters, your thoughts should be wholly directed to all that is true, all that deserves respect, all that is honest, pure, admirable, decent, virtuous, or worthy of praise.

Live according to what you have learned and accepted, what you have heard me say and seen me do.

Then will the God of peace be with you.

This is the Word of the Lord.

Response: Thanks be to God.

BROWN-ROA, a division of Harcourt Brace & Company

Eve of All Saints

General Intercessions

Celebrant:

God, our loving Father, we thank You for bringing us together as a family. We ask through Your Son, Jesus, to make us true followers of Jesus. We open our hearts to hear and listen to Your Word in our lives. Hear us as we pray.

Commentator:

Our response will be, "Lord, hear our prayer."

Eighth Grader:
For all Christians, that we may understand what it means to be one family in Jesus, let us pray to the Lord.

All: Lord, hear our prayer.

Seventh Grader:
For our parish family, that we may show by what we say and do that we are brothers and sisters in Christ, let us pray to the Lord.

All: Lord, hear our prayer.

Sixth Grader:
For the members of God's family who are lonely, sick, or suffering, let us pray to the Lord.

All: Lord, hear our prayer.

Fifth Grader:
For all the members of God's family who need our prayers, let us pray to the Lord.

All: Lord, hear our prayer.

Fourth Grader:
For our parents, God's first gift to us, let us pray to the Lord.

All: Lord, hear our prayer.

BROWN-ROA, a division of Harcourt Brace & Company

Third Grader:

For all children on Halloween that they may have a safe and happy day, let us pray to the Lord.

All: Lord, hear our prayer.

Second Grader:

For our pope, bishops, priests, and teachers and all people who lead us to follow Jesus, let us pray to the Lord.

All: Lord, hear our prayer.

First Grader:

For all the saints who are in heaven above, that we may ask them to shower us with love.

All: Lord, hear our prayer.

BROWN-ROA, a division of Harcourt Brace & Company

Eve of All Saints

Communal Thanksgiving

Commentator:

Pray a line at a time slowly. Children repeat the line after the commentator.

Take my body, Jesus . . .

Eyes and ears and tongue.

Never let them, Jesus, help to do Thee wrong.

Take my heart and fill it, full of love for Thee.

All I have I give Thee

Give Yourself to me.

BROWN-ROA, a division of Harcourt Brace & Company

Thanksgiving Liturgy

Theme:	Thanksgiving is a time to pause and recall our blessings and give thanks.
Entrance Procession:	Traditional (Seventh grader brings up thank you notes; sixth grader brings up Thanksgiving collage.)
Gathering Song:	"We Gather Together" (Missalette)
First Reading:	Tobit 12:6
Responsorial Psalm:	(See attached suggestion.)
Second Reading:	Colossians 3:15–17
Alleluia:	Verse of "Thank You, Lord," Carey Landry, *Hi God!*
Gospel:	Luke 17:11–19—the Ten Lepers
General Intercessions:	Petitions prayed with slide presentation
Preparation Hymn:	"Thank You, Lord," *Hi God!*
Gifts Procession:	Two children carry bread and wine.
Holy, Holy, Holy:	Missalette or *Hi God 2*
Memorial Acclamation:	"Christ has Died," Tim Schoenbachler, *Glory & Praise* 1
Amen:	"Lilies of the Field," *Reader's Digest*
The Lord's Prayer:	Missalette (Choose one familiar to parish)
Lamb of God:	Heritage Mass, Owen Alstot: Missalette
Communion Hymn:	"Come Along with Me to Jesus," Carey Landry, *Hi God 2*
Communal Prayer of Thanksgiving:	"Thank You for the World So Sweet" Sign Language (group in front of sanctuary)
Recessional Song:	"America the Beautiful" (traditional)

Preparation:

It seems to be a good idea to place the food donation at the altar before the celebration; otherwise, children play with cans during Mass and it can be distracting.

Children receive a flyer earlier in the week to invite them to share their food with needy persons.

Background music is played.

Children process into church about ten minutes before the celebration and, while directed by teachers, they place their gifts near the altar.

They return quietly to their assigned places and wait for the beginning of Mass.

While waiting they may listen to music, or take time to go over the songs to be used during the celebration.

After the Mass is celebrated, the confirmation candidates come forward, put the food in boxes, and place the boxes in a side room. Later, men from the St. Vincent de Paul collect the boxes and deliver the food to a needy family or parish.

Entrance Procession:

The seventh grader brings up thank-you notes. Later on, some of these "Thank you, God" notes may be put into the bulletin. If the child's name is used, it is well to ask the child's permission; otherwise, compile a Thanksgiving Litany without names, noting that the Litany is composed of children's Thanksgiving prayers.

The sixth-grade Thanksgiving collage may be placed on a wall or bulletin board after Mass to be enjoyed by other parishioners.

Thanksgiving Mass

Theme:

(to be read by a sixth grader):

Jesus, our Brother, you sat down to talk and eat with Your friends. You always reminded them to say thanks. We want to say "thank you" too, so we've come together today to celebrate. At this time of Thanksgiving, we ask Your help in discovering opportunities to say "thank you" to those we often overlook.

Opening Prayer:

(celebrant):

Did you ever stop to think about a tiny lady bug? The lady bug helps us by eating insects which harm our plants. Did you ever see a contact lens? It is so very small. But it helps us to see and read and learn. There are so many little things that we can say "thank you" for. And there are many big things too. Can you name some of the big things we are thankful for? (Allow children to respond if you would like.) There are so many things to be thankful for. Let us today learn to say thanks not only for the big things but the small too.

First Reading:

A reading from the book of Tobit: (12:6)

(to be read by a second grader):

Raphael called the two men aside privately and said to them: "Thank God! Give him the praise and the glory. Before all the living, acknowledge the many good things he has done for you, by blessing and extolling his name in song. Before all men, honor and proclaim God's deeds, and do not be slack in praising him." This is the word of the Lord.

All: Thanks be to God.

Reader:
Let us give thanks to the Lord. He is good to us. His love will last forever.

All: Let us give thanks to the Lord. He is good to us. His love will last forever.

Responsorial Psalm:

(to be read by a fifth grader):

Reader:
Let everyone in school know that God's love will last forever.

Let everyone on the streets know that God's love lasts forever.

BROWN-ROA, a division of Harcourt Brace & Company

Let everyone who works know that God's love lasts forever.

Let everyone who needs help know that God's love lasts forever.

All: Let us give thanks to the Lord. He is good to us. His love will last forever.

Reader:
When I was having a rough time in school and was failing, the Lord helped me to study. And later in life the Lord gave me the strength and courage to make many difficult and serious decisions. He has always helped and loved me.

All: Let us give thanks to the Lord. He is good to us. His love will last forever.

Reader:
With the Lord's help, we see that every day is a beautiful day worth living. Let us be happy and glad, for the Lord has been very good to us.

All: Let us give thanks to the Lord. He is good to us. His love will last forever.

Second Reading:

A reading from Paul's letter to the Colossians (3:15–17)

(second grader)

Dedicate yourselves to thankfulness. Let the word of Christ, rich as it is, dwell in you. . . . Sing gratefully to God from your hearts in psalms, hymns, and inspired songs. Whatever you do, whether in speech or in action, do it in the name of the Lord Jesus. Give thanks to God the Father through him. This is the Word of the Lord.

All: Thanks be to God.

Gospel:

Luke 17:11–19—The Ten Lepers

All: Praise to You, Lord Jesus Christ.

Homily:

Talk about the one leper being thankful and the rest forgetting to say thanks.

BROWN-ROA, a division of Harcourt Brace & Company

General Intercessions:	**Leader:** Please respond, "Thank You, Lord."
Celebrant:	Thank You, Lord for all our gifts: for food to share, for warmth, and sunshine. (Point out the gifts of food the children brought up before Mass.) May we continue to share ourselves and our food with others. Now let us bring our bread and wine that will soon be our food. Jesus welcomes us and comes to us in Holy Communion. Let us prepare in Thanksgiving by singing, "Thank You, Lord."
Gift Procession:	Kindergarten and first grader bring up bread and wine
Prayer after Communion:	(Pray after reader, line by line) Thank You for the world so sweet. Thank You for the food we eat. Thank You for the birds that sing. Thank You, God, for everything!
Suggestion:	One teacher taught the above prayer in sign language, and her class came forward to pray in sign language while she prayed aloud the words to the traditional prayer of thanks. **Blessing by Priest:** Go, children, and speak of Christ to others. Be happy to bring this joy to your friends. **All: Thanks be to God!**
Recessional Song: "America"	1. My country, 'tis of Thee, Sweet land of liberty, Of thee I sing; Land where my fathers died, Land of the pilgrims' pride, From every mountainside, Let freedom ring.

BROWN-ROA, a division of Harcourt Brace & Company

2. Our fathers' God, to Thee,
   Author of liberty,
   To Thee we sing;
   Long may our land be bright
   With freedom's holy light;
   Protect us by Thy might,
   Great God, our King.

Have a very happy Thanksgiving Day, especially since you have shared a gift for the poor.

Teachers and Staff

BROWN-ROA, a division of Harcourt Brace & Company

Thanksgiving

General Intercessions:

(Slides are suggested but not necessary.)

Leader:
Please respond, "Thank You, Lord."

Slide 1 (Baby)

In thanksgiving for the gift of life, let us pray to the Lord.

Response: Thank You, Lord.

Pause

Slide 2 (Sun)

In thanksgiving for the sun, moon, and stars, let us pray to the Lord.

Response: Thank You, Lord.

Pause

Slide 3 (People)

In thanksgiving for our family and friends, let us pray to the Lord.

Response: Thank You, Lord.

Pause

Slide 4 (People sharing meal)

In thanksgiving for all people to share food and shelter, let us pray to the Lord.

Response: Thank You, Lord.

Pause

BROWN-ROA, a division of Harcourt Brace & Company

Sukkoth—The Jewish Thanksgiving

Once again, we have erected a *Sukkah* in our church during this season of Thanksgiving. Some people have asked, "Why do we have a Jewish custom displayed in a Catholic church"? This is a valid question and the answer is: Most of our Christian feasts originated in the traditions of our Jewish ancestors. When we strive to be followers of Jesus, we try to understand the mind of Jesus as He lived our His life in union with His Father.

Because Jesus was a devout Jew, He celebrated the Feast of Sukkoth during the harvest time. This festival took place over eight days and was spent in the desert contemplating the Jews' heritage of slavery and hardship. They spent this "retreat time" reminding God of all He did for them in the past, asking for present favors, and thanking Him for all that had been given. The Feast of Sukkoth capsulizes the attitude of the Jew and thus the attitude of Jesus: "All that I am and all that I have, has been **given** to me by a God who is so gracious!" Humility and gratitude are thus the prevelant aspirations of Christians everywhere.

In many ways Sukkoth is similar to our American Thanksgiving, and some scholars believe the pilgrims, having read the story in the Bible, were inspired to celebrate their first Thanksgiving around the time of the Sukkoth festival.

The celebration of Sukkoth begins five days after the solemn feast of Yom Kippur and continues for eight days. It is customary among traditional Jews to build a booth in their yard, to decorate it with the fruits of the harvest, and to eat their meals in it for the eight-day festival. This is to commemorate the time when the Jews were traveling with Moses through the desert to the Promised Land. Therefore, the feast is also known as the Festival of Booths.

In conjunction with the study of the Old Testament, the sixth-grade class will be adding a Jewish flavor to their celebration of Thanksgiving. The class will participate in a prayer service for Thanksgiving which will incorporate a replica of a booth, otherwise known as a *Sukkah*. Our *Sukkah* will be on display in the front of the church from November 17 until the first Sunday of Advent.

BROWN-ROA, a division of Harcourt Brace & Company

Thanksgiving Prayer Service

Leader: My dear people, we have gathered together this day to tell the stories about the God who saved us, to praise Him, and give Him thanks. Let us take a moment to realize why we come to open our hearts to the God who is present in this celebration.

Entrance Procession: Cross bearer, servers, Moses, slaves, Indians, pilgrims, readers, celebrant

Gathering Song: "We Gather Together," Missalette

Opening Prayer: Celebrant

First Reading: Junior High student (Moses and slaves enter after this reading.)

Response Song: "Thank You, Lord" (refrain), Carey Landry, *Hi God!* (Children, Indians, pilgrims, other land children enter.)

Second Reading: Junior High student (Lincoln proclaims the Day of Thanksgiving to be set aside.)

Response Song: "Sing Out in Thanksgiving," Robert E. Kreutz and Willard F. Jabusch, *Glory & Praise* 3

Gospel: Matthew 15:32–39 (Jesus feeds the four thousand.)

Homily: Dialogue homily about gifts and thanks

Intercessory Prayers: Intermediate students

Slides: Scenes of nature, people, family thanksgiving (silence, with reflective music used in background)

Closing Prayer: Celebrant

Recessional Song: "America the Beautiful" (traditional)

Preparation:

Prepare a Junior High student to read the first reading.

Present an introduction to Moses. Moses will need a server's cassock and cane.

Select twelve seventh graders to represent slaves. Practice the chant beforehand. Choose ten primary graders to be pilgrims and Indians. Choose ten intermediate graders to represent persons from other lands. Pilgrims and Indians wear simple headbands; children from other lands wear simple clothes with different hats.

The seventh and eighth grade girls form a choir and, with the teacher, lead the songs. All participate in singing.

Thanksgiving Prayer Service

Call to Worship:
Celebrant:

God and Father of all gifts, we praise You, the source of all we have and are. Teach us to acknowledge always the many good things Your infinite love has given us. Help us to love You with all our heart and our strength. We ask this through Jesus Christ, Your Son, who lives and reigns with You and the Holy Spirit, one God, forever and ever.

All: Amen.

BROWN-ROA, a division of Harcourt Brace & Company

Thanksgiving Prayer Service

First Reading:

(Use microphone.)

A long time ago, in a far away land called Egypt, there lived a people named the Hebrews. Their lives were very hard because they were slaves working to build palaces for the king.

God looked down upon these people and took pity on them; so, He sent them a strong leader named Moses.

(Moses enter with slaves: Stand in front of altar, to the center.)

Moses helped these Hebrew slaves to escape from Egypt but they had to wander for forty years in the desert before they could find a place to call home.

Before they settled in Israel, the Promised Land, God wanted His people to always remember **who they were and what He had done for them so He told Moses.**

(Moses and slaves move to the side away from center.)

Group chants:
On the fifteenth day of the seventh month, when you have harvested the produce of the land, you are to celebrate the Feast of Sukkoth. On the first day, you shall take choice fruits, palm branches, and willows from the river bank. For seven days you are to live in shelters so that your descendants may know that I made the sons of Israel live in shelters when I brought them out of the land of Egypt. I am the Lord your God.

Response: "Thank You, Lord" (refrain), *Hi God!*

Second Reading:

(Indians, pilgrims, and foreign-land children enter and stand in center during Second Reading.)
(Use microphone.)

*(Lincoln with black top hat and beard reads **slowly and loudly**.)*

There is another story about people who were looking for a place to call home, a place where they could be free to worship God in their own way, to raise their children without poverty and disease, and to live free from hatred and prejudice. From England and Ireland, from Germany and Russia, from all over the world, they came. Some came in sailing vessels and some came in steamships. They came to live in our United States. It took many years for the young country of America to form a strong government, to gain independence from other countries who would want to rule her, but when freedom and prosperity were secured in 1813, President Lincoln declared:

BROWN-ROA, a division of Harcourt Brace & Company

The year that is drawing toward its close has been filled with the blessings of fruitful fields and heartful skies.

These bounties are so constantly enjoyed that we are prone to forget the Source from which they come.

I do, therefore, invite my fellow citizens in every part of the United States . . . to set apart and observe the next Thursday of November as a Day of Thanksgiving and Praise to our benevolent Father who dwells in the heavens.

(All children then take their seats in the assembly.)

Response Song:

Refrain of "Sing Out in Thanksgiving," Willard F. Jabusch and Robert E. Kreutz, *Glory & Praise* 3

Scripture:
Matthew 15:32–39

Homily:

Dialogue with assembly on some gift or gifts they are particularly grateful for this Thanksgiving.

Intercessory Prayers:

Response: Thank You, Lord.

Quiet Reflection:

Pray in silence.

Closing Prayer:

(Celebrant)

Gracious and loving God,
we thank You for all these blessings.
Help us to be truly grateful.
Help us to cherish freedom.
Help us to live the values our country is built on.
We ask this in the name of Jesus.
Amen.

BROWN-ROA, a division of Harcourt Brace & Company

Song:

America the Beautiful

O beautiful for spacious skies, for amber waves of grain,
For purple mountain majesties above the fruited plain.
America! America! God shed His grace on thee
And crown thy good with brotherhood from sea to
shining sea.

O beautiful for pilgrim feet, whose stern impassioned
stress,
A thoroughfare for freedom beat, across the wilderness.
America! America! God mend thine every flaw,
Confirm thy soul in self-control, thy liberty in law.

BROWN-ROA, a division of Harcourt Brace & Company

Thanksgiving Prayer Service

Intercessory Prayers:

(Grades four-six)

(Show slides of people, lands, mountains, Thanksgiving meals, beauty-of-nature scenes. Background music— ("This Land Is My Land" or "America the Beautiful" or "My Country, 'Tis of Thee" or reflective instrumental music.)

Please respond, "Thank You, Lord."

Grade Four:
For freedom of speech . . .
for freedom from want . . .
for freedom from fear . . .
for freedom of religion . . .
let us pray to the Lord.

Response: Thank You, Lord.

Grade Five:
For our president and leaders . . .
for peace and prosperity . . .
for justice, and equality . . .
for health of body and soul . . .
let us pray to the Lord.

Response: Thank You, Lord.

Grade Six:
For the beauty of nature . . .
for the blessings of living in this land of liberty . . .
for our rich heritage . . .
for the hope and peace we now enjoy . . .
let us pray to the Lord.

Response: Thank You, Lord.

BROWN-ROA, a division of Harcourt Brace & Company

Advent–Customs Prayer Services

The Advent Wreath

Advent Wreath Art:

Beforehand articles for making an Advent wreath should have been gathered: a round base, wire or styrofoam, some evergreens (preferably plastic), three purple candles and one pink candle, candle holders, and a bow. Assign children to take the various parts within the service.

Leader: Waiting for something important in our lives is both exciting and painful. Exciting because the coming event completes our dreams and hopes. Painful because the waiting takes time and allows us only to think and not experience the coming event. *Advent* means "coming". The coming of Jesus for the first time and every time. Once again, we celebrate the waiting for this wonderful event in the story of our journey to the Lord.

The symbol of our waiting is an Advent wreath which we will now assemble. (The children, previously prepared, now bring their part of the Advent wreath to the table and say their part.)

Child 1: The wreath in the shape of a circle symbolizes eternity.

Child 2: The evergreens are a sign of everlasting life.

Child 3: The purple candles remind us of penance and the pink candle of joy.

Child 4: The number of candles, four, stands for the four weeks in Advent and the thousands of years that the world waited for Jesus.

Leader: While we wait during these four weeks, we remember that Jesus desires to come into our lives, if we say "yes" to Him.
As we think about our preparing for His birthday, let us prayerfully bless our wreath.

Leader: Our help is in the Name of the Lord . . .

Children: Who has made heaven and earth.

BROWN-ROA, a division of Harcourt Brace & Company

Leader:	Let us pray. O God by whose Word all things are sanctified, pour forth Your blessing upon this wreath, and grant that we who use it may prepare our hearts for the coming of Christ and may receive from You abundant grace. Through Christ Our Lord.
Children:	Amen.
(Sprinkle the wreath with holy water as all sing "O Come, O Come, Emmanuel.")	*Focus on Living,* Teacher Manual, BROWN-ROA, 385–386.
Prayers of lighting the candles:	Each week one more of the candles is lit. A prayer is said at the lighting of the candle. The second week two candles are lit. The third week, three. The fourth week, all four. An Advent song is sung each time. The prayer which is said at the beginning of each week can be taken from the Introductory Prayer of that Sunday's Mass. While the candle(s) is being lighted, everyone may sing "O Come, O Come, Emmanuel."
First Sunday of Advent:	Stir up Your power, we beseech You, O Lord, and come: that from the threatening dangers of our sins, by Your protection we may deserve to be rescued, and be saved by Your deliverance: Who lives and reigns for ever and ever. Amen.
Second Sunday of Advent:	Stir up our hearts, O Lord, to prepare the ways of Your only-begotten Son; that through His coming we may attain to serve You with purified minds: Who lives and reigns for ever and ever. Amen.
Third Sunday of Advent:	Incline Your ear to our prayers, we beseech You, O Lord; and enlighten our minds by the grace of Your visitation: Who lives and reigns for ever and ever. Amen.
Fourth Sunday of Advent:	Stir up Your power and come, we pray You, O Lord; and with great might succor us; that the good which our sins impede, by the help of Your grace and the forgiveness of Your mercy, may speedily deliver us: Who lives and reigns for ever and ever. Amen.

BROWN-ROA, a division of Harcourt Brace & Company

The Jesse Tree

The Jesse Tree is a special reminder that the reason of Advent is a season of preparation and promise. A small evergreen or branch from any tree may be used to form the base of the Jesse Tree. The type of tree is not important. What is important is the special types of decorations that are hung on the tree.

The Jesse Tree is named for the father of the most famous Israelite king—David. Many years after Jesse and David lived, St. Matthew and St. Luke wrote that Jesus was born into their royal family. These ancestors, plus all the holy men and women of the Hebrew Scriptures, make up the spiritual background of Jesus. We count them all as part of Jesus' family tree.

Symbol:

Ark for Noah
Lamb for Isaac
Ladder for Jacob
Coat for Joseph
Burning bush for Moses
Harp for David
Crown for Solomon
Whale for Jonah
Dove for Elisha
Rose for Isaiah

Heart for Ruth
Wheel for Ezekiel
Lion for Daniel
Lily for Mary
Camel for Wisemen
Star for Wisemen

When we make a Jesse Tree, we remember the family of Jesse and all who helped prepare the world for the coming of Jesus. We think about one thing which will help us recall each person. For instance, an ark reminds us of Noah. A harp makes us think of David who played it and sang before the Lord. A lion reminds us of the prophet Daniel who was thrown into a lion's den for speaking the Word of God.

BROWN-ROA, a division of Harcourt Brace & Company

Jesse Tree symbols may be fashioned from all types of materials: colored paper, yarn, straws, pipe cleaners, and aluminum foil. Use your Bible to see why certain symbols remind us of certain people.

Biblical Reference:

Genesis 6:9–22
Genesis 22:1–19
Genesis 28:10–22
Genesis 37
Exodus 3
1 Samuel 16:14–23 (some translations say lyre)
1 Kings 1:11–48
Jonah 1
2 Kings 5:1–27 (spirit of healing)
Isaiah 35:1–2 (some translations say crocus)
Ruth 1:15–18
Ezekiel 1:15–21
Daniel 6:1–24
Traditional
Matthew 2:1–12
Matthew 2:1–12

Blessing the Jesse Tree:

O God, Your holy light has shone through the lives of prophets, priests, kings, and other holy people of the Old Testament as You prepared the world for the coming of Jesus Christ. Bless now this Jesse Tree, that it may remind us of Your past love and inspire us to praise You for the gift of love that You have given us in Your Son, our Savior, Jesus Christ. Amen

Focus on Relating, BROWN-ROA, 160.

BROWN-ROA, a division of Harcourt Brace & Company

Kristkindl

"Kristkindl" is another German custom. The word, "Kristkindl" means Christ Child. One way we can see and serve the Christ in others is through the "Kristkindle" custom. The practice is adaptable for all age groups and used frequently with the faculty or classroom students. The following are suggested directions.

1. Each person places his or her name on a slip of paper. Slips are collected into a box and each one draws a name. The name that you draw is your Kristkindl for Advent. Your Kristkindl is not to know who you are. You must be careful to keep the secret.

2. Each day you will do something "special" for your Kristkindl. It can be a special prayer or an act of service offered to him or her. Whatever you do for your Kristkindl, you must not get caught.

3. Each week you write a note or send a card to your Kristkindl telling of special prayers or acts offered for him or her, but do not sign it. Remember while you do this for another, someone is doing something similar for you.

4. At Christmas, when you write your final letter or card, sign it and let your Kristkindl know who you are. Sometimes small, inexpensive gifts are exchanged.

Suggestion: Some faculty members choose a "Kristkindl" at the beginning of the school year. The "Kristkindl" is remembered during the school year in surprise ways. At the closing gathering before summer, the persons exchange small gifts or wishes and let your "Kristkindl" know who you are. The idea is to keep a spirit of giving all year around.

BROWN-ROA, a division of Harcourt Brace & Company

The Mary Candle

God prepared His own Mother for His coming by creating her and keeping her without sin. God's preparation of Our Lady is clearly shown in the Feast of the Immaculate Conception. To help children understand the place of this feast in the liturgy, the making of a Mary candle is very symbolic.

Preparation for making the Mary candle can begin with a search through the Old Testament for titles which refer to Our Lady (Key of David, Root of Jesse, Ark of the Covenant, House of Gold, Tower of David). Once the titles have been found, symbols can be drawn to represent them.

Divide a tall white candle into four parts, as shown. In each part either paint or paste an already drawn symbol. Finally, the candle stick is draped with a white cloth, gathered and tied, like a "skirt."

Explain the symbolism involved: the **white candle,** the purity of Our Lady, the **white cloth,** the virginal flesh of Mary which Christ was formed; the **flame,** Mary's love which gives light and warmth to those weeks of preparing for the Birth of Jesus.

Many families gather around the lighted Mary Candle and pray the Hail Mary together. This is a simple but meaningful prayerful experience in keeping with Advent.

BROWN-ROA, a division of Harcourt Brace & Company

Ceremony for Gift Giving

Each Parish has its own tradition for giving gifts. Some adopt a hospital, or nursing home, others involve St. Vincent de Paul and other groups in delivering the gifts. Whatever way it is done, it is appropriate to include a simple ceremony which could take place in any appropriate place.

1. Begin with lighting the Advent wreath.

2. Sing an Advent hymn.

3. Offer your gifts one by one: each one carries his/her gift up to a table near the Advent wreath. (Adapt this process to Parish way of gathering gifts.)

4. End with reciting this prayer.

Prayer:
Hasten, we beseech You, O Lord and do not tarry, and grant us the help of Your heavenly power: that those who trust in Your goodness may be helped by the consolations of Your coming: Who lives and reigns forever and ever. Amen.

*Beforehand have containers set up, drivers assigned, and time to meet and deliver the gifts.

BROWN-ROA, a division of Harcourt Brace & Company

The "O Antiphons"

Come, Lord, and Do Not Delay!

The seven "O" Antiphons are an expression of the Church's anticipation of Christmas. They are seven liturgical chants or prayers, one for each day, from the evening of December seventeenth to December twenty-fourth. They express the Advent longing of all ages and are an important part of Christmas preparation.

December 17:
O Wisdom, who came out of the mouth of the Most High, reaching from end to end and ordering all things mightily and sweetly: come and teach us the way of prudence.

December 18:
O Adonai, and Leader of the House of Israel, who appeared to Moses in the flame of the burning bush, and gave to him the Law on Sinai: come and with an outstretched arm redeem us.

December 19:
O Root of Jesse, who stands for an ensign of the people, before whom kings shall keep silence, and to whom the Gentiles shall make their supplication: come to deliver us, and tarry not.

December 20:
O Key of David, and Sceptre of the House of Israel, who opens and no man shuts, who shuts and no man opens: come and bring forth from his prison-house, the captive that sits in darkness and in the shadow of death.

BROWN-ROA, a division of Harcourt Brace & Company

December 21:

O Dawn of the East, brightness of the light eternal, and Sun of Justice, come and enlighten those sit in darkness and in the shadow of death.

December 22:

O King of the Gentiles and the desired of them, Cornerstone that makes both one, come and deliver man, whom You formed out of the dust of the earth.

December 23:

O Emmanuel, Our King and Lawgiver, the expected of the nations and their Saviour, come to save us, O Lord our God.

There is a sense of rootedness and longing in the "O" Antiphons. Many teachers include the symbols in art and use the prayers to decorate the bulletin boards in classroom or Parish facilities. They can be added to daily prayer. They help create an atmosphere of preparation and longing for the coming of the Savior. In this way, it reinforces the true meaning of Advent.

BROWN-ROA, a division of Harcourt Brace & Company

First Sunday of Advent

Cycle C

Theme:	We prepare for Christ's birth through prayer, good works, and penance.
Entrance Procession:	Traditional
Gathering Song:	"O Come, O Come, Emmanuel" (Missalette)
Advent Wreath Blessing:	Celebrant lights first candle. He explains the symbolism and prays the First Sunday of Advent prayer blessing. (See attached.)
First Reading:	Jeremiah 33:14–16
Responsorial Psalm:	Psalm 25:4–5, 8–9, 10, 14
Second Reading:	1 Thessalonians 3:12–4:2
Alleluia:	Cantor: Psalm 85:8
All:	Alleluia (Missalette)
Gospel:	Luke 21:25–28, 34–36
Homily:	We prepare for the birth of the Lord.
General Intercessions:	Students
Preparation Hymn:	"Oh! How Good Is the Lord," Carey Landry, *Young People's Glory & Praise*
Gifts Procession:	Two children carry bread and wine.
Holy, Holy, Holy:	"Holy, Holy, Holy," *Hi God 2*
Memorial Acclamation:	"Christ Has Died . . ." (Missalette)
Amen:	"Lilies of the Field," *Reader's Digest*
The Lord's Prayer:	Missalette (Choose one familiar to parish)
Lamb of God:	Missalette (Choose one familiar to parish)
Communion Hymn:	"Hail Mary: Gentle Woman," Carey Landry, *Glory & Praise* 1
Recessional Hymn:	"Rejoice in the Lord Always," Carey Landry (Round), *Hi God!*

First Sunday of Advent

The Advent Wreath:

The wreath, a circle, is the symbol of eternity; the evergreens, of the eternal life and the immutability of God; the purple candles and ribbon, of penance; the pink candle, of the joy of Gaudete Sunday; and the number of candles, four, of the four weeks in Advent and the thousands of years that the world waited for the Redeemer.

(Saturday evening or the first Sunday of Advent the blessing of the Advent Wreath takes place.)

The Blessing:

Leader:
Our help is in the Name of the Lord . . .

All: Who hath made heaven and earth.

Leader:
Let us pray. O God, by whose Word all things are sanctified, pour forth Thy blessing upon this wreath, and grant that we who use it may prepare our hearts for the coming of Christ and may receive from Thee abundant grace. Through Christ our Lord.

(Sprinkle wreath with holy water.)

All: Amen.

After the blessing, the priest or leader reads the prayer for the first week of Advent and the first candle is lit. Each week a different prayer is said and another candle is lit so that by the fourth week of Advent all the candles are burning brightly. The prayer which is said at the beginning of each week can be taken from the Opening Prayer of that Sunday's Mass. While the candle is being lit, everyone may sing "Emmanuel."

First Sunday of Advent Prayer:

Stir up Your power, we beseech You, O Lord, and come: that from the threatening dangers of our sins, by Your protection we may deserve to be rescued, and be saved by Your deliverance: Who lives and reigns forever and ever. Amen

BROWN-ROA, a division of Harcourt Brace & Company

First Sunday of Advent

Cycle C

First Reading:

Jeremiah 33:14–16

A reading from the book of the prophet, Jeremiah.

The days are coming, says the Lord, when I will fulfill the promise I made to the house of Israel and Judah. In those days, in that time, I will raise up for David a just shoot: he shall do what is right and just in the land. In those days, Judah shall be safe and Jerusalem shall dwell secure; this is what they shall call her: "The Lord our justice."

This is the Word of the Lord.

Response: Thanks be to God.

Responsorial Psalm:

Psalm 25:4–5, 8–9, 10, 14

Response: To you, O Lord, I lift up my soul.
Your ways, O Lord, make known to me; teach me your paths.
Guide me in your truth and teach me, for you are God my savior, and for you I wait all the day.

Response: To you, O Lord, I lift up my soul.

Good and upright is the Lord:
Thus he shows sinners the way.
He guides the humble to justice,
He teaches the humble his way.

Response: To you, O Lord, I lift up my soul.

All the paths of the Lord are kindness and constancy
Toward those who keep his covenant and his decrees.
The friendship of the Lord is with those who fear him,
And his covenant, for their instruction.

Response: To you, O Lord, I lift up my soul.

BROWN-ROA, a division of Harcourt Brace & Company

First Sunday of Advent

Cycle C

Second Reading:

1 Thessalonians 3:12–4:2

A reading from the first letter of Paul to the Thessalonians.

May the Lord increase you and make you overflow with love for one another and for all, even as our love does for you. May he strengthen your hearts, making them blameless and holy before our God and Father at the coming of our Lord Jesus with all his holy ones.

Now, my brothers [and sisters], we beg and exhort you in the Lord Jesus that, even as you learned from us how to conduct yourselves in a way pleasing to God—which you are indeed doing—so you must learn to make still greater progress. You know the instructions we gave you in the Lord Jesus.

This is the Word of the Lord.

Response: Thanks be to God.

Alleluia:

Psalm 85:8 (cantor)

Alleluia. Lord, let us see Your kindness, and grant us Your salvation.

Response: Alleluia.

BROWN-ROA, a division of Harcourt Brace & Company

All Saints' Day

November 1

Theme:	Today we honor the saints and hope to join them one day.
Entrance Procession:	Saints (representatives from each grade level, with banner) enter with celebrant.
Gathering Song:	"When the Saints Go Marching In," *Reader's Digest or Focus on Music*
First Reading:	Revelation 7:2–4, 9–14
Responsorial Psalm:	"Isaiah 49," Carey Landry. *Glory & Praise* 1 (first verse and refrain)
Second Reading:	Parade of Saints (one representative from each grade)
Alleluia:	Missalette
Gospel:	Matthew 5:1–12
Homily:	Tell why we honor the saints; talk about our call to holiness.
General Intercessions:	Grades one through eight pray the petitions.
Preparation Hymn:	"Sing to the Mountains," Bob Dufford, *Glory & Praise* 1
Gifts Procession:	Two children (saints) carry bread and wine.
Holy, Holy, Holy:	"Holy, Holy, Holy," Carey Landry, *Hi God 2*
Memorial Acclamation:	"Christ has Died," music by Tim Schoenbachler, *Glory & Praise* 1
Amen:	"Lilies of the Field," *Reader's Digest*
The Lord's Prayer:	"The Lord's Prayer," Missalette
Lamb of God:	Recite, Missalette
Communion Hymn:	"Here I Am, Lord," Dan Schutte, *Glory & Praise* 3
Communal Thanksgiving:	Echo Prayer led by leader, with gestures.
Recessional Hymn:	"Blest Be the Lord," Dan Schutte, *Glory & Praise* 1

All Saints' Day

I [John] saw another angel come up from the east holding the seal of the living God. He cried out at the top of his voice to the four angels who were given power to ravage the land and the sea, "Do not harm to the land or the sea or the trees until we imprint this seal on the foreheads of the servants of our God." I heard the number of those who were so marked—one hundred and forty-four thousand from every tribe of Israel. . . .

After this I saw before me a huge crowd which no one could count from every nation and race, people and tongue. They stood before the throne and the Lamb, dressed in long white robes and holding palm branches in their hands. They cried out in a loud voice, "Salvation is from our God, who is seated on the throne, and from the Lamb!" All the angels who were standing around the throne and the elders and the four living creatures fell down before the throne to worship God. They said: "Amen! Praise and glory, wisdom and thanksgiving and honor, power and might, to our God forever and ever. Amen!"

Then one of the elders asked me, "Who are these people all dressed in white? And where have they come from?" I said to him, "Sir, you should know better than I." He then told me, "These are the ones who have survived the great period of trial; they have washed their robes and made them white in the blood of the Lamb.

This is the Word of the Lord.

Response: Thanks be to God.

BROWN-ROA, a division of Harcourt Brace & Company

All Saints' Day

Parade of Saints

Narrator: Today we celebrate the feast of All Saints! It is a time for celebration. People from all around the world, from all ages, from many walks of life now enjoy being in heaven. They were like you and me; they had good times and bad, joy and sorrow. They chose to love God and lived according to that choice. A few of the more famous saints are here to talk to you tonight/today.

St. Peter: I am Saint Peter. I was a fisherman. My brother Andrew introduced me to Jesus, and my life changed. I was chosen to be the leader of the apostles. Even though I three times denied knowing Jesus the night before he was crucified, he forgave me. I died on a cross, too. My feast day is June 29.

St. Matthew: I am Saint Matthew. I was a tax collector. The Jewish people did not like me, but Jesus chose me to be one of his apostles. I wrote the first Gospel. I died a martyr's death. My feast day is September 21.

Mary: I am Mary. I was born in Jerusalem. When I was a child, my parents took me to the temple where I promised my life to God. Later, God sent the angel Gabriel to ask me to be the mother of Jesus. I asked Jesus to perform his first miracle. At the cross, Jesus made me your mother, too. I have more than ten feast days, two of which are holy days.

St. Paul: I am Saint Paul. I was a Jewish tentmaker who persecuted Christians until Jesus appeared to me. My life changed and I carried the good news about Jesus to many people. I wrote letters to them that are now in your Bible. I was killed by the Emperor Nero for being a Christian. My feast day is June 29.

St. John: Hi! I am Saint John. I was a fisherman in Galilee. My brother James and I were called the Sons of Thunder by Jesus because we lost our tempers easily. I was the youngest of the apostles, and I saw many of Jesus'

BROWN-ROA, a division of Harcourt Brace & Company

miracles. I wrote the fourth Gospel. I was at the foot of the cross with Mary. My feast day is December 27.

St. Joseph: I am Saint Joseph. I was the foster father of Jesus. When he was a baby, I took him to Egypt and protected him from King Herod. I worked as a carpenter in Nazareth. I am the patron of workers. My feast days are March 19 and May 1.

St. Anne: I am Saint Anne. I am the grandmother who became a saint. My daughter's name is Mary and my grandson is Jesus. My feast day is July 26.

St. Vincent de Paul: Hello! I am Saint Vincent de Paul. I was born in France in 1580. I became a priest when I was 20. Later, I was captured by pirates and sold as a slave. After escaping, I returned to France where I worked to help the poor and started hospitals and orphanages. There is an organization in many parishes named after me. Each month there is a collection for those in the parish who are in need. My feast day is September 27.

St. Mark: I am Saint Mark. I was a follower of Jesus and traveled with Saint Paul on some of his missionary journeys. I wrote the second Gospel. My feast day is April 25.

St. John Vianney: I am Saint John Vianney, the saint to whom parish priests pray for help. I was a priest, too. I had much difficulty with my studies, but God helped me—He gave me a different gift to help people. It was insight into people's minds and souls. This enabled me to be a good spiritual director and help people in confession. My feast day is August 4.

St. Thérèse of Lisieux: I am Saint Thérèse of Lisieux. I was the youngest of nine children. My parents taught me about Jesus when I was very small. I learned to make presents of love out of everything—even sweeping the floor. That is how I got to be a saint. My nickname is The Little Flower of Jesus. My feast day is October 1.

St. Francis of Assisi: I am Saint Francis of Assisi. I had everything a young man could want, but I chose to give it all away to follow Jesus and help the poor. Other young men and women who wanted to live according to my rule joined me and became Franciscans. I started the custom of

putting out a Nativity scene at Christmas. I am also
know for my love of all God's creatures. My feast day is
October 4.

Narrator: Remember, you can be a saint, too—if you will just
follow Jesus in your life. And here ends our
presentation. (All exit.)

Barbara Bartley and Carol Wilson, *Children's Liturgies,*
BROWN-ROA, 137–138.

BROWN-ROA, a division of Harcourt Brace & Company

All Saints' Day

Celebrant:
We come to honor the saints. We, too, are called to holiness. Saints are happy people who live as followers of Jesus. Like the saints, let us pray in Jesus' name.

Petitions: Please respond, "Bless us and make us one."

1. For the love of the saints on this Holy Day that we may follow Jesus in a special way, we pray to the Lord.

2. For _____ Parish, great and small, young and old, that we follow God's call, we pray to the Lord.

3. For the homeless, the handicapped, for all people who need God's love, that God will send them special blessings from heaven above, we pray to the Lord.

4. For the followers of Jesus that we continue to follow Jesus' way, each and every day, we pray to the Lord.

5. For John Paul, our Pope, so he'll continue to pray for our world with great hope, we pray to the Lord.

6. For good health in our families, good will toward people, and that the Lord keeps us safe 'til we meet again, we pray to the Lord.

7. For all the saints and each one of us who are chosen from above to serve, help, smile, forgive one another, and show our love, we pray to the Lord.

8. For our confirmation classes that the Holy Spirit inspires our students as each day passes, we pray to the Lord.

BROWN-ROA, a division of Harcourt Brace & Company

Feast of the Immaculate Conception

December 8

Theme:	Today we honor Mary, the Mother of God, who was called from the very beginning and who answered "yes" to God.
Entrance Procession:	Traditional
Gathering Song:	"Immaculate Mary," Missalette (Sing the first two verses and the refrain. Light two Advent candles to be burned during the Mass.)
First Reading:	Genesis 3:9–15, 20
Psalm Response:	Psalm 98:1, 2–3, 3–4
Second Reading:	Ephesians 1:3–6, 11–12
Alleluia:	Missalette (Choose one familiar to parish)
Gospel:	Luke 1:26–38
Homily:	Mary responded "yes" to God. We, too, can say "yes" to God's call.
General Intercessions:	Grades four through eight pray petitions.
Preparation Hymn:	"Play Before the Lord," Bob Dufford, *Glory & Praise* 1
Gifts Procession:	Two children carry bread and wine.
Holy, Holy, Holy:	"Holy, Holy, Holy," *Hi God 2*
Memorial Acclamation:	"When We Eat This Bread," Carey Landry, *Glory & Praise* 1
Amen:	"Amen, Praise the Lord," *Kids' Praise 1*
The Lord's Prayer:	Missalette (Choose one familiar to parish)
Lamb of God:	Sung: Missalette (Choose one familiar to parish)
Communion Hymn:	"Hail Mary: Gentle Woman," Carey Landry, *Glory & Praise* 1
Recessional Hymn:	"O Come, O Come, Emmanuel," Missalette: verses 1,2,3 and refrain

Feast of the Immaculate Conception

December 8

First Reading:

Genesis 3:9–15, 20

Reader:
A reading from the book of Genesis . . .

[After Adam had eaten of the tree] the Lord God then called to the man and asked him, "Where are you?" He answered, "I heard you in the garden; but I was afraid, because I was naked, so I hid myself." Then he asked, "Who told you that you were naked? You have eaten, then, from the tree of which I had forbidden you to eat!" The man replied, "The woman whom you put here with me—she gave me fruit from the tree, and so I ate it." The Lord God then asked the woman, "Why did you do such a thing?" The woman answered, "The serpent tricked me into it, so I ate it."

Then the Lord God said to the serpent: "Because you have done this, you shall be banned from all the animals and from all the wild creatures. On your belly shall you crawl, and dirt shall you eat all the days of your life. I will put enmity between you and the woman, and between your offspring and hers. He will strike at your head, while you strike at his heel."

The man called his wife Eve, because she became the mother of all the living.

This is the Word of the Lord.

Response: Thanks be to God.

Responsorial Psalm:

Psalm 98:1, 2–3, 3–4

Cantor:

Sing to the Lord a new song, for he has done wondrous deeds.

All: Sing to the Lord a new song,
for he has done wondrous deeds.

1. Sing to the Lord a new song
for he has done wondrous deeds:

BROWN-ROA, a division of Harcourt Brace & Company

His right hand has won victory for him,
his holy arm. **R.**

2. The LORD has made his salvation known:
in the sight of the nations he has revealed his justice.
He has remembered his kindness and his faithfulness
toward the house of Israel. **R.**

3. All the ends of the earth have seen
the salvation by our God.
Sing joyfully to the Lord, all you lands;
break into song; sing praise. **R.**

Second Reading:
Ephesians 1:3–6, 11–12

Reader:
A reading from the letter of Paul to the Ephesians.

Praised be to God and Father of our Lord Jesus Christ, who has bestowed on us in Christ every spiritual blessing in the heavens: God chose us in him before the world began, to be holy and blameless in his sight, to be full of love; he likewise predestined us through Christ Jesus to be his adopted sons—such was his will and pleasure—that all might praise the glorious favor he has bestowed on us in his beloved.

In him we were chosen; for in the decree of God, who administers everything according to his will and counsel, we were predestined to praise his glory by being the first to hope in Christ.

Reader:
This is the Word of the Lord.

All: Thanks be to God.

Gospel:
Luke 1:26–38

Alleluia:
Luke 1:28

Cantor:
Alleluia

All: Alleluia

BROWN-ROA, a division of Harcourt Brace & Company

Cantor:
Hail, Mary, full of grace, the Lord is with you: blessed are you among women.

All: Alleluia

Comment before Communion:
Mary prepared herself for Jesus and each Communion prepares us for Jesus. Let us pray silently that Jesus will bring us His love and peace.

Comment after Communion:
We go forth from this Mass with a feeling of love. Because we know we received love, we can give more love. Let us follow the example of Mary who said "yes" to God.

BROWN-ROA, a division of Harcourt Brace & Company

Feast of the Immaculate Conception

General Intercessions

Petitions:	**Eighth grader:** Please respond, "Lord, hear our prayer." **Grade eight:** For the poor of the world, that they may be blessed by the generosity of people who care, we pray to the Lord. **Grade seven:** For the sick, the lonely, and the homeless that they will be comforted by the love of people who care for them, we pray to the Lord. **Grade six:** For our teachers, our priests, our staff, and students, that we may all prepare for Christmas by our spirit of kindness and love for each other, we pray to the Lord. **Grade five:** For peace in our world, peace in our families, and peace in our city, we pray to the Lord. **Grade four:** For ourselves, that we, like Mary, will always say "yes" to God, we pray to the Lord.

BROWN-ROA, a division of Harcourt Brace & Company

Feast of Our Lady of Guadalupe

December 12

Theme:	We come to celebrate on the Feast of Our Lady of Guadalupe.
Entrance Hymn:	"Amazing Grace," *Glory & Praise* 1 or Entrance Antiphon, Revelation 12:1
Opening Prayer:	From the Missal for the feast
First Reading:	Zachariah 2:14–17
Second Reading:	Revelation 11:19; 12:1–6, 10
Alleluia:	Missalette
Gospel:	Luke 1:39–47
Homily:	Story of Our Lady of Guadalupe
General Intercessions:	Students pray.
Preparation Hymn:	"Sing to the Mountains," Bob Dufford, *Glory & Praise* 1
Prayer Over the Gifts:	Missalette
Gifts Procession:	Children dressed in Indian shawls carry up water and wine.
Preface:	Preface of the Blessed Virgin Mary, I or II
Holy, Holy, Holy:	From *Hi God!*
Memorial Acclamation:	"When We Eat This Bread," Carey Landry, *Glory & Praise* 1
Amen:	"Amen," Erich Sylvester *Glory & Praise* 1
The Lord's Prayer:	Missalette: Recite
Lamb of God:	Missalette: Recite
Communion Hymn:	"Sing of Mary," or other Marian Song; or "One Bread, One Body," John Foley, *Glory & Praise* 2
Recessional Song:	"Hail Mary: Gentle Woman," Carey Landry, *Glory & Praise* 1

Our Lady of Guadalupe

December 12

First Reading:

A reading from the book of the prophet Zachariah

Sing and rejoice, O daughter Zion!
See, I am coming to dwell among you, says the Lord.
Many nations shall join themselves to the Lord on
that day, and they shall be his people, and
he will dwell among you, and you shall know
that the Lord of hosts has sent me to you.
The Lord will possess Judah as his portion
in the holy land, and he will again choose Jerusalem.
Silence, all mankind, in the presence of the Lord!
for he stirs forth from his holy dwelling.

This is the Word of the Lord.

Response: Thanks be to God.

BROWN-ROA, a division of Harcourt Brace & Company

Our Lady of Guadalupe

December 12

. . . God's temple in heaven opened and in the temple could be seen the ark of his covenant . . . A great sign appeared in the sky, a woman clothed with the sun, with the moon under her feet, and on her head a crown of twelve stars. Because she was with child, she waited aloud in pain as she labored to give birth. Then another sign appeared in the sky; it was a huge dragon, flaming red, with seven heads and ten horns; on his heads were seven diadems. His tail swept a third of the stars from the sky and hurled them down to the earth. Then the dragon stood before the woman about to give birth, ready to devour her child when it should be born. She gave birth to a son—a boy destined to shepherd all the nations with an iron rod. Her child was caught up to God and to his throne. The woman herself fled into the desert, where a special place had been prepared for her by God. . . .

Then I heard a loud voice in heaven say:
"Now have salvation and power come,
the reign of our God and the authority of his
Anointed One."

This is the Word of the Lord.

Response: Thanks be to God.

BROWN-ROA, a division of Harcourt Brace & Company

Our Lady of Guadalupe

December 12

General Intercessions

Prayer (celebrant):
God, our almighty Father, who wished that Mary, Your Son's mother, be celebrated by each generation, now in need we ask: Mary, full of grace, pray for us.

1. You made Mary the mother of mercy; may all who are faced with trials feel her motherly love, we pray.

R. Mary, full of grace, pray for us.

2. You wished Mary to be the mother of the family in the home of Jesus and Joseph; may all mothers of families foster love and holiness, we pray.

R. Mary, full of grace, pray for us.

3. You gave Mary strength at the foot of the cross and filled her with joy at the resurrection of Your Son; lighten our hardships and deepen our sense of hope, we pray.

R. Mary, full of grace, pray for us.

4. You made Mary open to Your word and faithful as Your servant; through her help make us servants and true followers of Jesus, we pray.

R. Mary, full of grace, pray for us.

5. You crowned Mary queen of heaven, may all the dead rejoice in Your kingdom with the saints forever, we pray.

R. Mary, full of grace, pray for us.

Prayer (celebrant):
On the Feast of Our Lady of Guadalupe, let us turn to Mary. Let us remember your appearance, Our Lady, to Juan Diego near Mexico City. Bless all of us. We honor you, Our Lady of Guadalupe, as Patroness of the Americas.

BROWN-ROA, a division of Harcourt Brace & Company

A Family Christmas Eucharistic Celebration

Theme:	We gather as a family to celebrate Jesus' birthday. Jesus is our greatest gift. Jesus, the Son of God, was born on Christmas Day. Jesus became one of us.
Entrance Procession:	Cross bearer, candle holders, children (angels) with halos, lector carrying lectionary high, priest celebrant carrying a large gift-wrapped box. The priest unwraps box slowly. He then holds the Infant Jesus statute high for all to see. He says, "Today is a day of giving: Jesus is our greatest gift." The angels then form around the altar until after the Gloria when they return to their families.
Gathering Song:	"O Come, All Ye Faithful," Missalette
Penitential Rite:	"Lord have mercy, Christ have mercy, Lord have mercy."
Gloria:	Leader directs the children in simple gestures while the Gloria is prayed. (Children return to families.)
First Reading:	Isaiah 62:1–5
Responsorial Psalm:	Psalm 96:1–2, 2–3, 11–12, 13
Second Reading:	(See prayer reflection on Nativity statues.)
Alleluia:	"Alleluia," Erich Sylvester *Glory & Praise* 1
Gospel:	Matthew 1:18–25 (short form)
Homily:	The birth of Jesus is a time of birthing and of exchanging gifts.
General Intercessions:	Students pray prayers of the faithful.
Preparation Hymn:	Christmas carols are sung.
Gift Procession:	A family carries bread, wine, candles, and chalice.
Eucharistic Prayer:	Eucharistic Prayer for Children 2
Holy, Holy, Holy:	*Hi God 2,* Carey Landry
Memorial Acclamation:	Christ has died, Christ has risen, Christ will come again.
Amen:	"Lilies of the Field," *Reader's Digest*

The Lord's Prayer: Missalette, recite, with joined hands.

Lamb of God: Missalette, recite

Communion Hymn: Christmas Carols

Recessional Hymn: (Two children carry birthday cake from back of the church. When they arrive near the altar, the congregation stands and sings, "Happy Birthday, Dear Jesus.")

Conclude with "We Wish You a Merry Christmas."

Christmas carols are played during recessional and after Mass.

A Christmas Celebration

Our manger is set up. Let us recall the story of Jesus' birth by looking at each statue.

First student: Mary
In our manger we see Mary. Mary is the mother of Jesus. Mary said "yes" to God's call to give birth to Jesus.

Second student: Joseph
Joseph, how good and just you are! You loved Mary and followed God's call. You placed your faith in God and helped prepare with Mary for Jesus' birth. You continued caring and loving.

Third student: Shepherds
How surprised you were to be led with your flocks over the fields to Jesus and to hear the good news: "A King will come and save us."

Fourth student: Animals
God must love animals very much. The animals were beside Jesus at His birth.

Fifth student: Angels
The angels proclaimed the good news of Jesus' birth, "Glory to God in the highest and peace to people of good will!"

Sixth student: Magi
The Magi journeyed long and far, following the star until it shone over the place where Jesus was born.

Seventh student:
On Christmas, we celebrate the birth of Jesus. God became human to live among us! We behold our infant Savior and celebrate His birthday.

BROWN-ROA, a division of Harcourt Brace & Company

A Christmas Celebration

Response, Come, Lord Jesus

1. For all families throughout the world that we may be open to receive God's gift of love, Jesus.

Come, Lord Jesus.

2. For all nations that they may receive the peace of Christ.

Come, Lord Jesus.

3. For the poor, the sick, and the lonely that they will receive God's care and love from others.

Come, Lord Jesus.

4. For all mothers and grandmothers that they may feel loved and cared for by their children.

Come, Lord Jesus.

5. For all fathers and grandfathers that they may be blessed with care and strength.

Come, Lord Jesus.

6. For all children that they may continue to be lights and joy to their friends and families.

Come, Lord Jesus.

7. Lord, help us to be Christians every day.

Come, Lord Jesus.

8. If you want to pray for someone, or for something else, please tell us and we will pray with you. As each person says an intention, all will reply:

"Come, Lord Jesus."

Priest:
Please, God, Our Father, grant all our petitions through Jesus Christ, Your Son and our brother.

All: Amen.

BROWN-ROA, a division of Harcourt Brace & Company

Gloria: Suggested Gestures

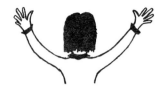

Glory be to God on high   (Hands raised)

And on earth peace to people of good will   (Peace sign)

We adore You.   (Hands folded high above head)
We praise You.

We Bless You.   (Hands outstretched above head in blessing)

We give You thanks for   (Hands above and high)
Your great glory.

Lord God, heavenly king,
God the Father almighty.   (slowly bring hands down.)

Lord, Jesus Christ,   (Hands joined at "Jesus Christ")
only begotten Son

BROWN-ROA, a division of Harcourt Brace & Company

Lord God, Lamb of God,
Son of the Father

(Keep hands joined.)

You who take away the sins of the world,
have mercy on us.

(Left arm across chest)

You who are seated at the right hand of the Father,
have mercy on us.

(Right arm crossing over left
arm on chest crisscross)

For You alone are the Holy One

(first)

You alone are the Lord.
You alone are the Most High.

(second)

Jesus Christ, with the Holy Spirit,
in the glory of God the Father. Amen.

(Hands joined.)

BROWN-ROA, a division of Harcourt Brace & Company

Solemnity of Mary, Mother of God

January 1

Theme: We celebrate the motherhood of the Virgin Mary, and worship her Son, Jesus Christ, the Lord.

Entrance Procession: Crossbearer, servers with candles, reader carrying lectionary high, and celebrant

Gathering Song: "Hail, Mary," Carey Landry, *Hi God 2*

First Reading: Numbers 6:22–27

Responsorial Psalm: "Sing a New Song," Dan Schutte, *Glory & Praise 1*

Second Reading: Galatians 4:4b–7

Alleluia: Hebrews 1:1–2

Gospel: Luke 2:15–21

Homily: Mary's role in God's saving plan.

General Intercessions: First through Fifth grades

Preparation Hymn: "O Come, All Ye Faithful," *Focus on Music* or Missalette—Christmas Issue

Gifts Procession: Two children carrying bread and wine

Holy, Holy, Holy: Missalette

Memorial Acclamation: "Christ Has Died," Missalette

Amen: "Amen," Erich Sylvester, *Glory & Praise 1*

The Lord's Prayer: Missalette, recite.

Lamb of God: Sung: Missalette (Choose one familiar to parish.)

Communion Hymn: "Hail Mary: Gentle Woman," Rev. Carey Landry, *Glory & Praise 1*

Recessional: "Joy to the World," *Focus on Music* or Missalette—Christmas Issue

Solemnity of Mary, Mother of God

First Reading:

A reading from the book of Numbers

The Lord said to Moses: "Speak to Aaron and his sons and tell them: This is how you shall bless the Israelites. Say to them: The Lord bless you and keep you! The Lord let his face shine upon you, and be gracious to you! The Lord look upon you kindly and give you peace! So shall they invoke my name upon the Israelites, and I will bless them."

This is the Word of the Lord.

Response: Thanks be to God.

Responsorial Psalm:
"Sing a New Song," Dan Schutte, *Glory & Praise*. 1

Second Reading:

A reading from the letter of Paul to the Galatians

. . . When the designated time had come, God sent forth his Son born of a woman, born under the law, to deliver from the law those who were subjected to it, so that we might receive our status as adopted sons. The proof that you are sons is the fact that God has sent forth into our hearts the spirit of his Son which cries out "Abba!" ("Father!"). You are no longer a slave but a son! And the fact that you are a son makes you an heir, by God's design.

This is the Word of the Lord.

Response: Thanks be to God.

Gospel

Luke 2:16–21

Celebrant:
Alleluia

Response: Alleluia.
Celebrant: In the past God spoke to our fathers through the prophets; now he speaks to us through his Son.

Response: Alleluia.

BROWN-ROA, a division of Harcourt Brace & Company

Solemnity of Mary, Mother of God

General Intercessions:

(Adapted from *Christian Prayer: The Liturgy of the Hours*)

Please respond: "Lord, grant us peace."

First Reader:
Blessed be the Lord Jesus, our peace, who came to unite us with God, let us pray to the Lord.

Response: Lord, grant us peace.

Second Reader:
When You were born You showed Your kindness and gentleness; help us always to be grateful for all Your blessings, let us pray to the Lord.

Response: Lord, grant us peace.

Third Reader:
You made Mary, Your Mother, full of grace; give all people the fullness of grace, let us pray to the Lord.

Response: Lord, grant us peace.

Fourth Reader:
You desired to become one of us by being born of the Virgin Mary; teach us to love each other in mutual respect, let us pray to the Lord.

Response: Lord, grant us peace.

Fifth Reader:
You came as the Sun rising over the earth, show the light of Your countenance to those who have died, let us pray to the Lord.

Response: Lord, grant us peace.

Priest or Leader:
God, our Father, may we profit by the prayers of the Virgin Mother Mary, for You bring us life and salvation through Jesus Christ her Son who lives and reigns with You and the Holy Spirit, one God, forever and ever.

Response: Amen.

BROWN-ROA, a division of Harcourt Brace & Company

Catholic Schools Week

Theme:	We come to celebrate Catholic Schools Week. As we share our gifts and talents, we thank God for our Catholic faith in this Eucharistic celebration.
Entrance Procession:	Traditional, with eighth graders carrying lighted candles.
Gathering Song:	"Sing a New Song," Dan Schutte, *Glory & Praise* 1
Prayer:	(See celebrant prayer.)
First Reading:	Isaiah 63:7–9
Responsorial Psalm:	"Rejoice in the Lord Always," *Hi God!* (3 times)
Second Reading:	Philippians 1:3–11 (Thanksgiving Prayer)
Alleluia:	"Alleluia," Erich Sylvester, *Glory & Praise* 1
Gospel:	Luke 17:11–19 (Reader reads while children pantomime the Ten Lepers and the one who comes back to say "Thanks.")
Homily:	What does it mean to have a Catholic heritage? How do gratitude and thanksgiving tie into a true spirit in school?
General Intercessions:	Students pray petitions.
Preparation Hymn:	"God Is So Good," Carey Landry, *Glory & Praise* 2
Gifts Procession:	Kindergarten through third graders carry bread and wine.
Holy, Holy, Holy:	"Holy, Holy, Holy," Carey Landry, *Hi God 2*
Memorial Acclamation:	"Christ Has Died, Christ Has Risen, Christ Will Come Again."
Amen:	"Lilies of the Field," *Reader's Digest*
The Lord's Prayer:	Missalette: recite
Lamb of God:	"Peace I Leave You," Carey Landry, *Glory & Praise* 3
Communion Hymn:	"We Come to Your Table," Carey Landry, *Hi God 2*
Recessional Hymn:	"The Spirit is A-Movin'," Carey Landry, *Glory & Praise* 1

Catholic Schools Week

Theme:

We gather together to celebrate Catholic Schools Week. We come to share our talents and express our love and faith in this celebration of the Eucharist. We pause this day in **this thanksgiving for one another.**

Opening Prayer:

(Celebrant)

Good and loving God, You fill us with your Spirit who strengthens us to do Your work. Through the example of Your saints, inspire us anew. Make us holy!

Help us to serve one another and so become an inspiration, a source of the Spirit, for all whom we encounter in Your name.

We ask this through Jesus Christ our Lord.

Response: Amen.

Presentation of Gifts:

Bread and wine will be presented by representatives from kindergarten, first, second, and third grades.

Communal Thanksgiving:

A school song: A representative from each homeroom will approach the altar to form the shape of a heart while the song is being sung.

Eucharistic Ministers:

Principal, DRE, and teachers.

Altar Servers:

Seventh Grade: Please assign.

(Those participating in special roles for this liturgy will

be called for practice _____ this week.)

                                              Date   Time

BROWN-ROA, a division of Harcourt Brace & Company

Catholic Schools Week

Let me sing the praises of Yahweh's goodness,
and of his marvelous deeds,
in return for all that he has done for us
and for the great kindness he has shown us
in his mercy and in his boundless goodness.

He said, "Truly they are my people, sons and no rogues."
He proved himself their savior in all their troubles.
It was neither messenger nor angel
but his Presence that saved them.
In his love and pity he redeemed them himself,
he lifted them up, carried them, throughout the days of old.
But they rebelled, they grieved his holy spirit.

This is the word of the Lord.

Response: Thanks be to God.

BROWN-ROA, a division of Harcourt Brace & Company

Catholic Schools Week

I thank my God whenever I think of you; and every time I pray for all of you, I pray with joy, remembering how you have helped to spread the Good News from the day you first heard it right up to the present. I am quite certain that the One who began this good work in you will see that it is finished when the Day of Christ Jesus comes. It is only natural that I should feel like this toward you all, since you have shared the privileges which have been mine: both my chains and my work defending and establishing the gospel. You have a permanent place in my heart, and God knows how much I miss you all, loving you as Christ Jesus loves you. My prayer is that your love for each other may increase more and more and never stop improving your knowledge and deepening your perception so that you can always recognize what is best. This will help you to become pure and blameless, and prepare you for the Day of Christ, when you will reach the perfect goodness which Jesus Christ produces in us for the glory and praise of God.

This is the word of the Lord.

Response: Thanks be to God.

BROWN-ROA, a division of Harcourt Brace & Company

Catholic Schools Week

Gospel:

Luke 17:11–19
(The Ten Lepers)

Now on the way to Jerusalem he traveled along the border between Samaria and Galilee. As he entered one of the villages, ten lepers came to meet him. They stood some way off and called to him, "Jesus! Master! Take pity on us." When he saw them he said, "Go and show yourselves to the priests." Now as they were going away they were cleansed. Finding himself cured, one of them turned back praising God at the top of his voice and threw himself at the feet of Jesus and thanked him. The man was a Samaritan. This made Jesus say, "Were not all ten made clean? The other nine, where are they? It seems that no one has come back to give praise to God, except this foreigner." And he said to the man, "Stand up and go on your way. Your faith has saved you."

This is the word of the Lord.

Response: Thanks be to God.

BROWN-ROA, a division of Harcourt Brace & Company

Catholic Schools Week

One day Jesus did a favor for ten people. He healed them. He forgave them. He made them better.

Do you know why Jesus was very pleased with one of the ten?

One day as Jesus was walking, He heard voices calling Him. Then He saw, standing a bit away from Him, ten people with a terrible skin disease. They were called lepers.

"Jesus, Master, take pity on us!" they cried.

Jesus looked at them with love. He said, "Go and show yourselves to the priest." As they turned away to do what Jesus said, their skin became like new again.

One of the ten, a stranger, turned back and threw himself at Jesus' feet. He cried, "Thank You, thank You, thank You!"

Jesus asked, "Where are the others? Weren't all ten of you cured? Where are the other nine? Is it only a stranger who came back to say thanks?"

"Go on your way. Your faith has made you whole today." (See Luke 17:11–19.)

This is the word of the Lord.

Response: Thanks be to God.

Celebrating the Gift of Forgiveness, BROWN-ROA, 47–48.

BROWN-ROA, a division of Harcourt Brace & Company

Catholic Schools Week

Celebrant:
God gives us the gift of life.

Our life is a sign of God's love for the world.

Let us turn to God in prayer for the world and for all those in need of God's love.

Response:
Lord, hear our prayer.

First Student: Eighth Grader
That the love of God we celebrate this day might be our Church's greatest legacy to the world, let us pray to the Lord.

Second Student: Seventh Grader
That the Light of Christ may guide all Christians to the unity and full communion which is God's will for us, let us pray to the Lord.

Third Student: Sixth Grader
That the nurturing gifts of life, love, and education which we receive from our parents might be our gift to all who look to us for strength and courage, let us pray to the Lord.

Fourth Student: Fifth Grader
That all who minister in the work of Catholic Education might be inspired by Christ's dedication to the Father's will, let us pray to the Lord.

Fifth Student: Fourth Grader
That the sick and grieving, the homeless and oppressed, might be freed from the darkness of their pain by the light of Christian communities dedicated to serving the needy, let us pray to the Lord.

Celebrant:
Gracious Lord, You sent Your Son, Jesus, as an example of loving service.

BROWN-ROA, a division of Harcourt Brace & Company

May we follow His example and be Your gift to one another and to those in need.

Let us pray to the Lord.

Response:
We ask this in the Name of Jesus Christ, Our Lord.

Response: Amen.

BROWN-ROA, a division of Harcourt Brace & Company

Candlemas Day: Feast of the Presentation of the Lord

February 2

Theme:	We celebrate the Feast of the Presentation of the Lord. Mary and Joseph, in fulfillment of the law, present Jesus in the temple. The prophecy was fulfilled that Simeon would see the Lord.
Blessing of Candles and Procession:	Missalette
Gathering Song:	"Hail Mary, Gentle Woman," Carey Landry, *Glory & Praise* 1
First Reading:	Malachi 3:1–4
Responsorial Psalm:	Psalm 24: 7, 8, 9, 10
Alleluia:	Missalette
Gospel:	Luke 2:32
General Intercessions:	Students pray the prayers.
Preparation Hymn:	"God Is So Good," Carey Landry, *Glory & Praise* 3
Holy, Holy, Holy:	Dufford, Schulte, *Glory & Praise* 1
Memorial Acclamation:	Christ has died, Christ has risen, Christ will come again.
Amen:	Amen (Missalette)
The Lord's Prayer:	"The Lord's Prayer," Erich Sylvester, *Glory & Praise* 1
Lamb of God:	Recite
Communion Hymn:	Luke 2:30–31 (chanted)
Recessional Hymn:	"I Have Loved You," Michael Joncas, *Glory & Praise* 2

Candlemas Day

First Reading:

Malachi 3:1–4

Lo, I am sending my messenger
to prepare the way before me;
And suddenly there will come to the temple
the Lord whom you seek
And the messenger of the covenant whom you desire.

Yes, he is coming, says the Lord of hosts.
But who will endure the day of his coming?
And who can stand when he appears?
For he is like the refiner's fire,
or like the fuller's lyre.

He will sit refining and purifying (silver)
and he will purify the sons of Levi

Refining them like gold or like silver
that they may offer due sacrifices to the Lord.
Then the sacrifice of Judah and Jerusalem
will please the Lord
as in days of old, as in years gone by.

Candlemas Day

Responsorial Psalm:

Psalm 24:7, 8, 9, 10

R. Who is this king of glory? It is the Lord!

Lift up, O gates, your lintels;
reach up, you ancient portals,
that the king of glory may come in!

R. Who is this king of glory? It is the Lord!

Who is this king of glory?
The Lord, strong and mighty,
the Lord, mighty in battle.

R. Who is this king of glory? It is the Lord!

Lift up, O gates, your lintels;
reach up, you ancient portals,
that the king of glory may come in!

R. Who is this king of glory? It is the Lord!

Who is this king of glory?
The Lord of hosts; he is the king of glory.

R. Who is this king of glory? It is the Lord!

BROWN-ROA, a division of Harcourt Brace & Company

Candlemas Day

Please respond:
Lord, hear our prayer:

First Student:
For our holy Father, the Pope, that He will guide the Church in love and peace, let us pray to the Lord.

Second Student:
For priests and religious that they may show their love and dedication in God's service, let us pray to the Lord.

Third Student:
For our teachers and faculty members that they may be strengthened by God's power and light to witness to God's loving care, let us pray to the Lord.

Fourth Student:
For our parents who work hard and sacrifice for us, let us pray to the Lord.

Fifth Student:
For students everywhere that they may renew their baptismal promises and follow Jesus closely, let us pray to the Lord.

Sixth Student:
For the sick and homebound that Jesus' light will bring them hope, let us pray to the Lord.

Seventh Student:
For all here present, that God will strengthen and give them peace, let us pray to the Lord.

BROWN-ROA, a division of Harcourt Brace & Company

Feast of St. Blaise

February 3

(Based on Fourth Sunday of Ordinary Time)

Theme: We gather together in this Eucharistic celebration to celebrate the Feast of St. Blaise. May Christ's power strengthen and nourish us along the way.

Entrance Procession: Traditional

Gathering Song: "Praise to the Lord," Joachim Neander, Missalette

First Reading: Zephaniah 2:3; 3:12–13

Responsorial Psalm: Psalm 146:6–7, 8–9, 9–10

Second Reading: 1 Corinthians 1:26–31

Alleluia: Missalette

Gospel: Matthew 5:1–12 (Beatitudes)

General Intercessions: Students pray.

Blessing: Procession and throat blessing takes place.

Preparation Hymn: "Path of Life," Mike Balhoff, *Glory & Praise* 3

Gifts Procession: Two children carry bread and wine.

Holy, Holy, Holy: Missalette

Memorial Acclamation: Christ has died, Christ has risen, Christ will come again. (Missalette)

Amen: Missalette

The Lord's Prayer: Missalette, recited

Communion Hymn: "Jesus, Jesus!" or "Oh How I Love Jesus!," Carey Landry, *Hi God!*

Recessional Hymn: "Bless, O Lord, Your People," Joe Pinson, *Glory & Praise* 3

St. Blaise

First Reading:

Zephaniah 2:3; 3:12–13

A reading from the book of the prophet Zephaniah.

Seek the Lord, all you humble of the earth,
  who have observed his law;
Seek justice, seek humility;
  perhaps you may be sheltered
  on the day of the Lord's anger.
But I will leave as a remnant in your midst
  a people humble and lowly,
Who shall take refuge in the name of the Lord:
  the remnant of Israel.
They shall do no wrong
  and speak no lies;
Nor shall there be found in their mouths
  a deceitful tongue;
They shall pasture and couch their flocks
  with none to disturb them.

This is the word of the Lord.

Response: Thanks be to God.

Responsorial Psalm:

Psalm 146:6–7,
8–9, 9–10

Response: Happy the poor in spirit. The kingdom of heaven is theirs.

[The Lord] keeps faith forever,
secures justice for the oppressed,
gives food to the hungry.
The Lord sets captives free.

Response: Happy the poor in spirit. The kingdom of heaven is theirs.

The Lord gives sight to the blind.
The Lord raises up those that were bowed down;
the Lord loves the just.
The Lord protects strangers.

Response: Happy the poor in spirit. The kingdom of heaven is theirs.

BROWN-ROA, a division of Harcourt Brace & Company

The fatherless and the widow he sustains,
but the way of the wicked he thwarts.

The Lord shall reign for ever;
your God, O Zion, through all generations.

Response: Happy the poor in spirit. The kingdom of heaven is theirs.

Second Reading:

1 Corinthians 1:26–31

A reading from the First Letter of Paul to the Corinthians.

Brothers (Sisters), you are among those called. Consider your own situation. Not many of you are wise, as men account wisdom; not many are influential; and surely not many are well-born. God chose those whom the world considers absurd to shame the wise; he singled out the weak of this world to shame the strong. He chose the world's lowborn and despised, those who count for nothing, to reduce to nothing those who were something; so that mankind can do no boasting before God. God it is who has given you life in Christ Jesus. He has made him our wisdom and also our justice, our sanctification, and our redemption. This is just as you find it written, "Let him who would boast, boast in the Lord."

This is the word of the Lord.

Response: Thanks be to God.

Response: Alleluia, alleluia, alleluia.

BROWN-ROA, a division of Harcourt Brace & Company

St. Blaise

General Intercessions:

Celebrant:
Let us now pray for those who are sick and suffering, for those who care for the sick, and for all who seek the blessing of good health. Please respond: Lord, hear our prayer.

Eighth Grader:
For those who suffer from sickness and disease, that they may receive healing, we pray to the Lord.

Seventh Grader:
For the mentally ill and for their families, we pray to the Lord.

Sixth Grader:
For those with physical disabilities and handicaps, that Christ may be glorified in their weakness, we pray to the Lord.

Fifth Grader:
For doctors and nurses, and for all who care for the sick, we pray to the Lord.

Fourth Grader:
For those who seek the prayers of St. Blaise today, that they may be protected from afflictions of the throat and other forms of illness, we pray to the Lord.

Teacher:
For our community sick and shut-ins. For . . ., we pray to the Lord.

Celebrant:
God our Father, your Son Jesus Christ looked upon the sick and healed them. Through the intercession of St. Blaise protect us from all sickness and disease. We ask this. . . .

Response: Amen.

BROWN-ROA, a division of Harcourt Brace & Company

Lenten Season: Ash Wednesday

Theme: We come together to celebrate the beginning of the forty days of Lent. Lent is a time of growth, a time of penance, and prayer. It is a time to follow Jesus more closely.

Entrance Procession: Cross bearer, altar servers carrying candles, lector holding book high, and priest celebrant.

Gathering Song: "Here I Am, Lord," Dan Schutte, *Glory & Praise* 3 (verses one and two, and refrain)

First Reading: Joel 2:12–18

Responsorial Psalm: Psalm 51:3–4, 5–6, 12–13, 14, 17

Second Reading: 2 Corinthians 5:20, 6:2

Gospel Acclamation: Psalm 51:12, 14 (omit if not sung)

Gospel: Matthew 6:1–6, 16–18

Ashes: Blessing and Imposition of Ashes (antiphon recited)

General Intercessions: Students

Preparation Hymn: "Hosea," by Gregory Norbet, OSB, *Glory & Praise* 3, or *Listen* (Weston) (verses one and two, and refrain)

Gifts Procession: Two students carry bread and wine.

Holy, Holy, Holy: Missalette

Memorial Acclamation: Christ has died, Christ has risen, Christ will come again—Missalette

Amen: Danish Amen—Missalette

Canon: Canon for children, #1., Children's Lectionary

The Lord's Prayer: Missalette, recite.

Sign of Peace: Handshake

Breaking of Bread: Lamb of God is recited.

Communion Hymn: "Blest Be the Lord," Dan Schutte, *Glory & Praise* 1 (antiphon and verse one)

Recessional Hymn: Instrumental Music or Lenten background music

Ash Wednesday

Readings

First Reading:

Joel 2:12–18

A reading from the book of the prophet Joel.

Even now, says the Lord,
 return to me with your whole heart,
 with fasting, and weeping, and mourning;
Rend your hearts, not your garments,
 and return to the Lord, your God.
For gracious and merciful is he,
 slow to anger, rich in kindness,
 and relenting in punishment.
Perhaps he will again relent
 and leave behind him a blessing,
Offerings and libations
 for the Lord, your God.
Blow the trumpet in Zion!
 proclaim a fast,
 call an assembly;
Gather the people,
 notify the congregation;
Assemble the elders,
 gather the children
 and the infants at the breast;
Let the bridegroom quit his room,
 and the bride her chamber.
Between the porch and the altar
 let the priests, the ministers of the Lord, weep,
And say, "Spare, O Lord, your people,
 and make not your heritage a reproach,
 with the nations ruling over them!
Why should they say among the peoples,
 'Where is their God?' "
Then the Lord was stirred to concern for his
 land and took pity on his people.

This is the Word of the Lord.

Response: Thanks be to God.

BROWN-ROA, a division of Harcourt Brace & Company

Responsorial Psalm:

Psalm 51:3–4, 5–6,
12–13, 14, 17

Response: Be merciful, O Lord, for we have sinned.

Have mercy on me, O God, in your goodness;
    in the greatness of your compassion wipe out my
    offense.
Thoroughly wash me from my guilt and of my sin
    cleanse me.

Response: Be merciful, O Lord, for we have sinned.

For I acknowledge my offense,
    and my sin is before me always:
"Against you only have I sinned,
    and done what is evil in your sight."

Response: Be merciful, O Lord, for we have sinned.

A clean heart create for me, O God,
    and a steadfast spirit renew within me.
Cast me not out from your presence,
    and your holy spirit take not from me.

Response: Be merciful, O Lord, for we have sinned.

Give me back the joy of your salvation,
    and a willing spirit sustain in me.
O Lord, open my lips,
    and my mouth shall proclaim your praise.

Response: Be merciful, O Lord, for we have sinned.

Second Reading:

2 Corinthians 5:20–6, 2

A reading from the second letter of Paul to the Corinthians.

We are ambassadors for Christ, God as it were appealing through us. We implore you, in Christ's name: be reconciled to God! For our sakes God made him who did not know sin to be sin, so that in him we might become the very holiness of God.

As your fellow workers we beg you not to receive the grace of God in vain. For he says, "In an acceptable time I have heard you; on a day of salvation I have helped you." Now is the acceptable time! Now is the day of salvation!

This is the Word of the Lord.

Response: Thanks be to God.

BROWN-ROA, a division of Harcourt Brace & Company

Ash Wednesday

General Intercessions:

Celebrant:
God's Word calls us to forgiveness and love. As one Body in Christ, let us offer our petitions for all who look to us for forgiveness and love.

Response: Lord, hear our prayer.

Eighth Grader:
For the leaders of our government, especially for our president, that they may work always for peace in the world, let us pray to the Lord.

Seventh Grader:
For parents, that their love for their children may help them grow in patience and kindness, let us pray to the Lord.

Sixth Grader:
For those who are sick, especially for the members of our parish, that the Lord will heal them with his love, let us pray to the Lord.

Fifth Grader:
For the students, that their love for one another may create undying memories that will bring them comfort throughout life, let us pray to the Lord.

Fourth Grader:
For our Holy Father, Pope John Paul, and the bishops of our Church that they may help the community of the Church remember the loving kindness God has shown us, let us pray to the Lord.

Third Grader:
For administrators and teachers in our schools, that their love for their students may never fail, let us pray to the Lord.

Second Grader:
For all of us, that we follow Jesus more closely, let us pray to the Lord.

BROWN-ROA, a division of Harcourt Brace & Company

First Grader:
For peace and love, let us pray to the Lord.

Celebrant:
God of Love, You call us out of darkness and You give us the grace to respond to Your call. Grant that we may follow Jesus closely during this special time of prayer and penance. Send Your Holy Spirit to direct our ways. Make us one Body in Christ through Jesus Christ our Lord.

Response: Amen.

BROWN-ROA, a division of Harcourt Brace & Company

Holy Thursday: Passover

I. **Introduction**

II. **Explanation of the Passover**

III. **Play**

    A. Evil leaders plotting Jesus' death with Judas

    B. Apostles and Jesus discussing where to celebrate the Passover Meal

    C. The Last Supper

    D. Jesus and Apostles at the Mount of Olives (End with Jesus' arrest.)

IV. **Litany of Thanksgiving**

Holy Thursday: Passover

I. Introduction:

H

Reader 1:
We are gathered here today to celebrate Jesus' sharing of Himself with us. Let us put aside our distractions as we listen to the explanation of the Passover Feast. (Pause)

II. Explanation of the Passover:

 Charlotte

H

Sam

Reader 2:
Jesus and His Apostles were like a family. They loved one another. Jesus and the Apostles were Jews. Like all Jews everywhere, they ate a special meal each year during the Passover. At this meal they remembered how God long ago had worked through Moses to free the Jews from slavery. The Jews had to leave Egypt in such a hurry that they could not take yeast for their bread. So the bread at the Passover Meal is unleavened.

Holy Thursday was Jesus' last celebration of the Passover. Let us go back to the time when Jesus was living, about two thousand years ago.

Caiphas and leaders with Judas.

III. Play:

Esther

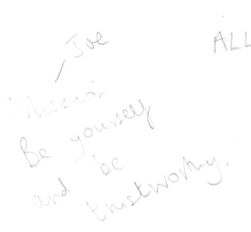
Joe

Be yourself
and be
trustworthy.

ALL

Reader 3:
This scene takes place at the residence of Caiphas, the High Priest. The evil leaders are plotting with Judas. They are plotting Jesus' death.

Reader 3:
Judas said, "What will you give me if I turn him over to you?"

Reader 4:
The evil leaders responded, "We will give you thirty pieces of silver."

Reader 4:
From that time on, Judas kept looking for an opportunity to hand Jesus over. The High Priests were fearful of arresting Jesus during the Passover celebration. They were worried that the people would riot.

BROWN-ROA, a division of Harcourt Brace & Company

Reader 5:
Soon after, on the first day of the Passover ceremonies, the disciples came to Jesus and asked,

Reader 6:
"Where shall we plan to eat the Passover Meal?"

Apostles and Jesus discussing where to celebrate the Passover Meal

Reader 5:
Jesus replied,

Reader 6:
"As soon as you enter Jerusalem, you will see a man walking along carrying a pitcher of water. Follow him into the house he enters, and say to the man who lives there, "Our teacher says for you to show us the guest room where he can eat the Passover Meal with his disciples. He will take you upstairs to a large room all ready for us. This is the place. Go ahead and prepare the meal there." So John and Peter went ahead to prepare the meal.

Reader 7:
Jesus went to the house where the Passover Meal was served. There he greeted the disciples as they entered the room, and he washed their feet, as a symbol that all of us are to serve and care for others. While he was doing this, John and Peter put a cloth on the table. They lit the candles and brought flowers for the celebration. They put out the bread to eat and the wine to drink.

Jesus and apostles gather around table/altar for Last Supper. (Pantomime)

Reader 8:
Jesus said, "I have looked forward to this hour with deep longing, anxious to eat this Passover Meal with you before my suffering begins. (Pause) One of you at this table will betray me."

(Jesus)

Reader 9:
Each of the disciples asked in disbelief, "Lord, am I the one?"

Reader 8:
Jesus replied, "It is one of you twelve eating with me now."

BROWN-ROA, a division of Harcourt Brace & Company

Reader 9:

As they were eating, Jesus took a small loaf of bread and blessed it and broke it apart, and gave it to his disciples and said,

Reader 8:

"Take this and eat it, for this is my body, given for you. Eat it in remembrance of me."

Reader 9:

Then he took a cup of wine and gave thanks to God for it and gave it to them saying:

Reader 8:

"Each one drink from it, for this is my blood, sealing the new agreement between God and man. I solemnly declare that I shall never again taste wine until the day I drink a different kind in the Kingdom of God. (Pause)

Reader 9:

When the Supper had ended, they all sang a hymn, and went out to the Mount of Olives.

Jesus and apostles at the Mount of Olives

Please join us in singing (choose familiar communion thanksgiving song.)

Reader 10:

When they arrived at the Mount, Jesus said,

Reader 11:

"Tonight your faith in me will be shaken. As written in the Old Testament, the Shepherd will be killed, and the sheep will scatter. But after I am raised to life again, I will go to Galilee and meet you there."

Reader 10:

And Peter replied, "Though all may have their faith in you shaken, mine will never be shaken."

Reader 11:

And Jesus said, "Before the cock crows at dawn, you will deny me three times."

Reader 10:

When Jesus and his apostles arrived in the Garden of Gethsemane, Jesus said to them.

BROWN-ROA, a division of Harcourt Brace & Company

Reader 11:

"Stay here, while I go and pray. My heart is nearly broken with sorrow. Remain here and stay awake with me."

Reader 10:

Jesus went on a little further and dropped to his knees and prayed.

Reader 11:

"Father, if it is your will, take this cup from me. Yet not my will, but yours be done."

Reader 10:

Two more times Jesus returned and found his apostles asleep. Finally he said,

Reader 11:

"Sleep on now; enjoy your rest! (Pause) But no! The time for sleep has ended! The hour is on us when the Son of Man is to be turned over to the power of evil men. Come! Get up! We must go! (Pause) Look! My betrayer is here!

Reader 10:

At this, Judas arrived with a great crowd carrying swords and clubs. Judas identified Jesus with a signal— an embrace. At this moment, they stepped forward and arrested Jesus. Peter immediately took a sword and cut off the ear of the high priest's servant. Jesus came forward, healed the ear and said,

Reader 11:

"Put back your sword where it belongs. Those who use the sword are sooner or later destroyed by it. (Pause) Am I some dangerous criminal that you had to arm yourselves with swords and clubs before you could arrest me? I was with you teaching daily in the Temple, and you didn't stop me then.

Reader 10:

At that point, all the disciples deserted him and fled.

BROWN-ROA, a division of Harcourt Brace & Company

Celebration of Interdependence and Unity

Theme:	Coming from diverse backgrounds and bringing our own uniqueness, we are called to unity and interdependence in Christ Jesus.
Call to Worship:	We are all different. We feel different. We look different. We think differently. We all talk and walk differently. Each one of us has to make up his or her own mind about things. Underneath, however, we are all one. We all belong to one another. We are a community.
Gathering Song:	"Peace Is Flowing Like a River," Carey Landry, *Hi God 2*
Entrance Procession:	Cross bearer, servers, children from first through eighth grade carrying poles with different color class-named streamers and eight more children carrying flower favors (The favors will be taken to persons in elderly persons home.), reader carrying lectionary high, and celebrant.
First Reading:	Genesis 11:1–9
Responsorial Song:	To the tune of "This Land Is Your Land," chorus (traditional)
Second Reading:	Acts 2:1–17
Alleluia:	"Alleluia," Erich Sylvester, *Glory & Praise* 1
Gospel:	Matthew 28:16–20
Homily:	We are called to unity and interdependence as disciples of Jesus Christ.
General Intercessions:	Spoken first in foreign language, then repeated in English.
Preparation Hymn:	"Yes, Lord, Yes!," Carey Landry, *Hi God 2*
Gifts Procession:	Children carry bread and wine.
Holy, Holy, Holy:	Missalette
Memorial Acclamation:	"When We Eat This Bread," Bob Dufford, *Glory & Praise* 1

Amen:	"Amen," Erich Sylvester, *Glory & Praise* 1
The Lord's Prayer:	"The Lord's Prayer," Erich Sylvester, *Glory & Praise* 1
Lamb of God:	Missalette, recite.
Communion Hymn:	"What a Friend We Have in Jesus," *Reader's Digest*
Post Communion Reflection:	Slide presentation (scenes from school, showing children and community experiences).
Recessional Hymn:	"This Land is Your Land" (traditional)
Preparation:	• Each class is given a colored streamer and long pole. Each child signs his/her name on the colored streamer. When completed, the streamer is attached to a long pole.

• Each class representative carries the class streamer pole in the entrance procession.

• The children form in a line on the altar, representing all the different children and lands. Before returning to their places, they place their poled color streamer into a specified container. The many-colored streamers decorate the sanctuary as a reminder of our uniqueness and unity.

• Flower favors or plants are purchased or made ahead of time. Eight children carry their flower favor. Each child places a favor on or near the altar. After the Mass celebration, the flower favors are brought to a specified nursing center or elderly home as a reminder of our reach-out interdependence.

Margaret Brennan, RSM, St. Bernardine School, Forest Park, IL.

Celebration of Interdependence and Unity

Preparation Hymn: **"Yes, Lord, Yes!"** Carey Landry

Verse one:
Children, children, will you come and follow me?
Will you come and follow me now?
Will you come and be an apostle of mine,
Will you come and follow me now?

Chorus:
Yes, Lord, Yes
Yes, Lord, Yes
Yes, Lord, we will come and follow you,
Follow you wherever you go.

Verse two:
Children, children, will you come and follow me,
Will you come and follow me now?
Will you come and help me spread the Good news?
Will you come and follow me now?

Copyright © 1976 North American Liturgy Resources,
Phoenix, Arizona 85029. All rights reserved.

Recessional Hymn: **"This Land is Your Land"**

Chorus:
This land is your land.
This land is my land,
From California
To the New York Island,
From the Redwood Forest
To the gulf stream waters,
This land was made for you and me.

Verse one:
As I was walking
That ribbon of highway,
I looked above me,
There is the skyway.
I looked below me
In the golden valley.
This land was made for you and me.

BROWN-ROA, a division of Harcourt Brace & Company

Chorus:

Verse two:
I followed your low hills
And I followed your cliff rims,
Your marble canyons
And sunny bright waters.
This voice came calling
As the fog was lifting . . .
This land was made for you and me.

BROWN-ROA, a division of Harcourt Brace & Company

Celebration of Interdependence and Unity

General Intercessions:

Four children representing different lands (adapt to parish needs) pray petitions. First, read in foreign language, then in English. Please respond, "Lord, help us to love."

First child:
(Representing other land)
Foreign: For people who need people
English: For people who need people, let us pray to the Lord.

R. English: Lord, help us to love.

Second child:
Foreign: For all the seniors
English: For all the seniors, let us pray to the Lord.

Third child:
Foreign: For all the people who do not know that they need others
English: For all the people who do not know that they need others, let us pray to the Lord.

Fourth child:
Foreign: For all the people in the world
English: For all the people in the world, let us pray to the Lord.

BROWN-ROA, a division of Harcourt Brace & Company

Confirmation Inscription Ceremony

Theme:	We gather as Church, People of God, to initiate our confirmation candidates.
Celebrant Prayer:	Recall baptism and bless water.
Rite of Sprinkling and Prayer for Forgiveness:	Missalette
Penance:	Lord have mercy. Christ have mercy. Lord have mercy.
Celebrant Prayer:	(Thanks for the Sacrament of Confirmation. Encourage candidates to enter more deeply into the life of the Church.)

Liturgy of the Word

First Reading:	Genesis 17:1–8 (Student)
Responsorial Psalm:	Missalette
Second Reading:	Deuteronomy 5:2–4 (Student)
Alleluia:	Choose one familiar to parish.
Gospel:	John 14:14–27
Homily:	What it means to renew our baptismal promise and live out our Christian commitments to follow Jesus.
Profession of Faith:	Renewal of Baptismal Promises. Please respond, "I do."

Rite of Inscription

Adults Renewal of Confirmation:	Please respond, "We do."
Commentator:	(Direct the candidates to move forward and sign Inscription Promises.)
Celebrant Prayer:	Missalette
Final Blessing:	Missalette
Conclusion:	Join hands and pray or sing the "Our Father."
Concluding Song:	Instrumental music played while leaving

Celebrant and staff are available for questions.

Initiation of Confirmation Candidates

Commentator:

Today is the day we receive the eighth grade members of our parish family as candidates for the Sacrament of Confirmation. With the Sacrament of Confirmation, they will enter a new stage of membership in the Church and in our community. Please stand and join the candidates in singing "Amazing Grace." *(Glory & Praise* 1)

Celebrant:

Today, we welcome the Class of _____ as they come to enroll as candidates for the Sacrament of Confirmation. They want to reaffirm their baptism. They want to deepen the bonds that bind us together in this community, that bind us together in the Church and in Christ. Let us then begin by recalling our own baptism. As this water is blessed, may it remind us of our baptismal promises. Let us pray.

Lord our God, bless this water. It is the sign of baptism, the sacrament that brings us new life in Jesus. May we always remember that we are called to share that life. Grant that, in sharing the new life we received in baptism, we may be made one in the Spirit that calls us to holiness, through our Lord Jesus Christ.

All: Amen.

Celebrant:

As we receive this blessed water, let us renew our commitment to our baptism and our faith.

(All present are blessed with the sprinkled water.)

Let us now call to mind those times that we somehow failed to commit ourselves to our families, our friends, and our classmates.

For the times that we were selfish with our time and help, we pray: Lord, have mercy.

All: Lord, have mercy.

For the times that we lacked the maturity to respond as the Christians we are called to be, we pray: Christ, have mercy.

BROWN-ROA, a division of Harcourt Brace & Company

All: Christ, have mercy.

For the times that we chose the "easy way" when living up to our commitments required strength and courage, we pray: Lord, have mercy.

All: Lord, have mercy.

Celebrant: May Almighty God have mercy on us, forgive us our sins, and bring us to life everlasting.

All: Amen.

Celebrant: Let us pray. Father, we Your people thank You for always renewing us. Thank You for the generosity and goodness of our candidates for the Sacrament of Confirmation. We delight in their creativity and their energy; we are happy that they want to use their gifts in the spirit of Your Son, Jesus. We encourage them to enter more deeply into the life of the Church. Grant them strength and courage. We ask this through Christ our Lord.

All: Amen.

BROWN-ROA, a division of Harcourt Brace & Company

Liturgy of the Word

First Reading:
Genesis 17:1–8

(student)

Responsorial Psalm
Response: Lord, send out your Spirit, and renew the face of the earth.

Bless the Lord, my soul!
Lord God, how great you are!
How many are your works, O Lord!
The earth is full of your riches!

Response: Lord, send out your Spirit, and renew the face of the earth.

You take back your Spirit, and they die, returning to the dust from which they came. You send forth your Spirit, and they are created, and you renew the face of the earth.

Response: Lord, send out your Spirit, and renew the face of the earth.

May the glory of the Lord last forever!
May the Lord rejoice in his works!
May my thoughts be pleasing to him.
I find my joy in the Lord.

Response: Lord, send out your Spirit, and renew the face of the earth.

Second Reading:
Deuteronomy 5:2–4

Gospel Acclamation:

The Father will send you the Holy Spirit, says the Lord, to be with you forever.

All: Alleluia

Gospel:
John 14:14–27

BROWN-ROA, a division of Harcourt Brace & Company

Profession of Faith

Renewal of the Baptismal Promises:

Celebrant:
Candidates for the Sacrament of Confirmation: You have already received the life of Christ. You received it when you were baptized. At that time, your parents, or godparents, made promises for you; they spoke in your name. We now invite you to reaffirm your baptism. You have each decided to present yourselves as candidates for another Sacrament of Initiation: the Sacrament of Confirmation.

Through the Sacrament of Confirmation we reaffirm our baptism. Now that you have grown to a new maturity in Christ, you can speak in your own name. It is, therefore, most fitting that the same promises you made at baptism be renewed as a way of presenting yourselves as candidates for confirmation.

(Candidates respond "I do" to each question.)

Celebrant:
Do you reject Satan?

Candidates:
I do.

Celebrant:
And all his works?

Candidates:
I do.

Celebrant:
And all his empty promises?

Candidates:
I do.

Celebrant:
Do you believe in God, the Father Almighty, creator of heaven and earth?

Candidates:
I do.

BROWN-ROA, a division of Harcourt Brace & Company

Celebrant:

Do you believe in Jesus Christ, His only Son, our Lord, who was born of the Virgin Mary, was crucified, died, and was buried, rose from the dead, and is now seated at the right hand of the Father?

Candidates:

I do.

Celebrant:

Do you believe in the Holy Spirit, the holy catholic Church, the communion of Saints, the forgiveness of sins, the resurrection of the body, and life everlasting?

Candidates:

I do.

Celebrant:

This is our Faith. This is the Faith of the Church. We are proud to profess it, in Christ Jesus our Lord.

Candidates:

Amen.

BROWN-ROA, a division of Harcourt Brace & Company

Rite of Inscription

Celebrant:

The faith we have just proclaimed is a gift . . . a gift from God. We are strengthened to assemble as a Church by the grace of the Spirit.

As the Church, we are all receivers of the gifts of the Spirit: understanding, right judgment, courage, knowledge, reverence, wonder, and awe in God's presence.

These gifts are to be shared. We welcome these candidates for the Sacrament of Confirmation. We are happy to share with them the gifts of the Spirit.

We are also happy to receive these candidates into fuller membership in the Body of Christ. We are all members in His Body. We have been made one with Him through the Sacrament of Baptism . . . a Sacrament of Initiation.

Today our eighth grade students are presenting themselves to receive their one remaining Sacrament of Initiation: Confirmation. They want to become fuller members of our parish and the Body of Christ. We are happy and proud to welcome them today as candidates for this sacrament.

Will all present who have already been confirmed, please stand and respond "We do" as we officially welcome our candidates.

Celebrant:

Do you understand that the gifts of the Spirit are given us for the good of the whole Church?

All: We do.

Do you therefore accept these members of our parish as candidates for the Sacrament of Confirmation?

All: We do.

Do you promise them your support in their program of preparation?

All: We do.

BROWN-ROA, a division of Harcourt Brace & Company

Do you promise to share in their preparation for this sacrament by your prayers, your encouragement, and your example?

(Please be seated.)

All: We do.

Celebrant:

Candidates for the Sacrament of Confirmation: Our parish has invited you to present yourselves as candidates who will more fully become members of the Body of Christ. Do you accept our invitation? Only you can decide to present yourselves for this candidacy.

You are about to declare yourselves ready to prepare for and receive the Sacrament of Confirmation. You will enter a new stage of membership in the parish and in the Church universal. For our part, we stand ready with prayerful help and support, as we now accept you as candidates for confirmation.

Stand

(Candidates respond "We do" to each question.)

Celebrant:

Do you understand that you are entering a program that will lead you to a deeper commitment as a member of the Church?

Candidates: We do.

Do you realize that we, the Church, require you to participate in a program of preparation?

Candidates: We do.

Do you willingly enter into this agreement with the parish, eager to cooperate in and participate in this program of preparation for the Sacrament of Confirmation?

Candidates: We do.

Do you realize that the gifts of the Holy Spirit are to be used for the service of others?

Candidates: We do.

Celebrant: Thanks be to God.

(Be Seated)

BROWN-ROA, a division of Harcourt Brace & Company

Commentator:

Each of us will be asked to sign our Commitment Promise. Today we received our Confirmation Booklet. They need to be completed. In the months ahead, they will serve as a reminder that we have accepted the challenge of commitment. When we return to our places, we will ask our parents or another adult to sign our commitment pledge. They will support you along the way. We have pledged ourselves to God, to our parish, and to our whole Church. On the day of confirmation, our finished booklets and journals will be a visible sign of the covenant that we have entered. We ask those present to witness our Inscription Promises and our signature pledge.

(The Candidates move forward and sign their Inscription Promises.)

Celebrant:

In the name of _____ Parish, I accept your Commitment Promises and bless your promises. (Candidates hold up booklets.) I hereby recognize each of you as a candidate for the Sacrament of Confirmation. I ask all present to join with me in prayer for you in the coming months as you prepare for the commitment you have made today.

Let us now return to our places and then invite our parents or adult witnesses to sign our pledges.

BROWN-ROA, a division of Harcourt Brace & Company

Final Blessing

Celebrant: May Almighty God bless you and send you forth to do His bidding.

All: Amen.

May His Spirit strengthen you to serve your families, your friends, and your parish.

All: Amen.

May Almighty God bless you, the Father, and the Son, and the Holy Spirit.

All: Amen.

Conclusion: Invite all the community to join hands as a visible sign of our unity and support as we join the candidates along the way to the Sacrament of Confirmation.

Conclusion Song: Sing or pray the "Our Father."

BROWN-ROA, a division of Harcourt Brace & Company

Confirmation Contract

I, _____

of _____

Agree to:

1. Cooperate to the best of my ability with the parish program preparing me for the Sacrament of Confirmation;

2. Participate in the classes and activities, and try to the best of my ability to place my talents at the service of others;

3. Pray for growth in faith, hope and love;

4. Strive for greater maturity;

5. Accept more responsibility in my family, my Church, and my community.

I ask the help of the Father, the Son, and the Holy Spirit in this agreement.

Signature: _____

Witnessed by parents: _____

Witnessed by teacher: _____

Date: _____

BROWN-ROA, a division of Harcourt Brace & Company

Parish Expectations of the Confirmation Candidates

Confirmation candidates must show a readiness for the sacrament by fulfilling the following parish expectations:

1. Each candidate shall strive to conduct him/herself as a Christian at school, at home, and in outside activities.

2. Each candidate will make prayer a special part of his/her life, especially by the practice of *regular* Sunday Mass attendance.

3. Each candidate will develop an awareness of his/her dependence on God for spiritual healing through participation in the Rite of Reconciliation.

4. Each candidate is responsible for knowing the basic prayers and doctrines of our faith.

5. Each candidate will undertake a service project and keep a record of it. The project involves finding ways to respond to the needs of the people around them (parish, community, school, home) during the entire year.

6. Each candidate will have an interview with one of the members of the parish staff, or a member of the parish community. During the interview, the candidate and the interviewer will discuss how he/she has carried out these parish expectations, the service project, his/her understanding of the meaning of confirmation and his/her desire to receive the Sacrament, or not, at this time. Appointment time will be assigned for the interviews.

7. Each candidate is to have a sponsor and meet with him/her several times during the year.

8. Each candidate is expected to participate in an all-day retreat.

9. Parents are invited to attend parent meetings.

10. Each candidate will commit himself/herself to furthering his/her Catholic religious training.

Candidates for confirmation must qualify for the sacrament by fulfilling the above parish expectations.

BROWN-ROA, a division of Harcourt Brace & Company

Confirmation Reconciliation Service

Theme: We as confirmation candidates are called to be witnesses of the Church and to show the love of God to all people.

Opening Song: "Peace is Flowing Like a River," Carey Landry, *Glory & Praise* 1

Call to Worship: See handout

Reflective Music: Musician's choice

Gospel: A story from the Gospel of Mark (See Mark 10:17–22.)

Examination of Conscience: See handout

Reflection: See handout

Act of Contrition: See handout

Individual Confession

Prayer of Penitent: (Personal Prayer)

Concluding Music: Instrumental music is played.

A Celebration of Reconciliation

Call to Worship:

(Leader)

My brothers and sisters, each of us has been chosen by God to play an important role in the Church. You and I are to be such witnesses to the love God has for all people that we help to transform the world into a most sacred place.

During our daily lives however, we do not always act as we should. In fact, we knowingly and willingly act against the moral law. We sin. The sinner is a person who fails in love of God or others. We must be aware of sin in our own lives. We must recall our failures and be truly sorry for them. Sorrow must inspire us to turn away from our selfishness toward God and His love.

We ask the Lord Jesus to give us His Spirit as we gather this evening to recall our sins, our confusion, and our guilt. As we listen to the Word of God in Scripture, we pray for mercy, understanding, and love. Above all, we pray for healing.

Reflection:

Reflective music on forgiveness.

Introduction to the Gospel:

(Celebrant)

A story from the Gospel of Mark.

One day Jesus was setting out on a journey and a young man came running up, knelt down before him and asked, "Good Teacher, what must I do to be your disciple?" Jesus said, "Why do you call me good? No one is good but God alone. You know the commandments, follow them." The young man replied, "Teacher, I have kept all these since my childhood." Then Jesus looked at him with great love and told him, "There is one thing more you must do. Go and sell what you have and give to the poor. After that, come and follow me." At these words, the young man's face fell. He went away sad, for this was too much!

BROWN-ROA, a division of Harcourt Brace & Company

Examination of Conscience:

What is my relationship to God?
Do I worship Him?

Do I pray often, do I celebrate Mass on Sunday?

Do I ask God for His help and trust His guidance?

Am I grateful to be a follower of Jesus and do I show it in my actions?

What is my relationship to myself?
Do I treat myself respectfully?

Do I care for my body by refraining from alcohol or drugs?

Do I care for my mind by studying and using the talents God has given me?

Do I care for my soul by nourishing my spirit with prayer, with quiet times, with receiving Holy Communion, and with receiving the Sacrament of Reconciliation?

Do I give into discouragement and moodiness?

Do I respect every part of my body as good?

What is my relationship to others?
Do I speak with reverence and act respectfully to parents and persons in authority?

Do I speak with reverence to my classmates, refrain from swearing, lying, fighting, gossiping, and name calling?

Do I respect others' property, refrain from destroying property, from stealing and cheating?

Do I help to make my surroundings (home, school) a happier place to live?

Do I serve others cheerfully? When was the last time I did a job for someone without being asked?

Do I look at sex as a beautiful part of creation, or do I make sex a plaything—reading and looking at cheap movies, acting out of selfishness, and treating others as cheap rather than as persons to respect and want as friends—true, honest, and faithful?

BROWN-ROA, a division of Harcourt Brace & Company

Reflect Silently:

What is one fault in your life that you want to change? What makes me fail? Is it pride? (I'm not asking God for help?)

Is it greed? (I like to have as much as I can.)

Is it envy? (I give into feelings of sadness when someone is praised or honored.)

Is it jealousy? (I think someone is getting more attention than myself.)

Is it sloth? (I am too lazy to go to church, do my chores, help out.)

If you have trouble ask Father to help you.

All pray: We have sinned against you, Lord. We have also sinned against one another. We are sorry for the harm and hurt we have caused. We ask for Your help so that we may grow more like You, loving and serving one another as You loved and served us.

A Celebration of Reconciliation:

An Act of Contrition:
My God, I am sorry for my sins with all my heart.
In choosing to do wrong and failing to do good,
I have sinned against You whom I should love above all things.
I firmly intend with Your help,
To do penance,
To sin no more,
And to avoid whatever leads me to sin.

Amen.

Individual Confession and Absolution:

Individual confessions:
(Celebrant)

Each candidate now confesses his/her sins to a priest of their choice.

As you wait for your brothers and sisters to receive the Lord's forgiveness, look for these passages in the Bible.

BROWN-ROA, a division of Harcourt Brace & Company

Luke:	6:17–26	Matthew:	5:1–12	John:	14:18–31
	6:27–38		16:24–28		15:1–8
					15:9–17

Romans:	6:1–14	Ephesians:	2:1–16	I John:	3:1–24
	6:15–23		4:1–17		4:7–21
	7:14–25		4:17–32		
	8:26–32				
	8:31–39	Colossians:	3:1–17		
	12:1–2, 9–21				

I Corinthians 13:1–13

After Confession and Absolution:

(Pray silently) Lord Jesus, bless each one of us. Help us all to feel Your love for us and help us to show our love to those around us. Help us always to remember that the most important thing in life is to live by Your commandment—"Love one another as I have loved you." Amen.

Say the Lord's Prayer.

Reflect on the penance the priest gives and how you will do it.

BROWN-ROA, a division of Harcourt Brace & Company

Confirmation Vigil Ceremony

Preparation Service for Candidates and Sponsors

Theme:	You have been chosen and God is well pleased. Ask God's Spirit—what do you **need** from Him?
Opening Song:	"To Jesus Christ Our Sovereign King," Missalette
Opening Prayer:	Missalette
Reading:	Isaiah 42:1–4
Meditation:	See handout
Reading:	Romans 8:14–17
Meditation:	From *That Man Is You*—Louis Evely
Gospel:	Luke 4:16–22
Homily:	"Our Church Needs You"
Presentation of Gifts:	Teachers are called forward to receive a religious memorable gift.
Sponsors' Blessing:	See handout
Practice and Directions:	Candidates and Sponsors
Closing Song:	"Holy God, We Praise Thy Name" (Missalette), or other song chosen by Celebrant

Confirmation Vigil

Opening Song: "To Jesus Christ, Our Sovereign King"

To Jesus Christ, our sovereign King,
Who is the world's salvation,
All praise and homage do we bring
And thanks and adoration.

Refrain:
Christ Jesus, Victor! Christ Jesus, Ruler!
Christ Jesus, Lord and Redeemer!

Your reign extend, O King benign,
To ev'ry land and nation;
For in your kingdom, Lord divine,
Alone we find salvation. Refrain

To you and to your Church, great King,
We pledge our heart's oblation;
Until before your throne we sing,
In endless jubilation. Refrain

Reading: Isaiah 42:1–4

Meditation:

1. How do you feel knowing you have been chosen by God, and He is "well pleased" with you? Speak to Him about this.

2. As you think about your confirmation tomorrow night, what do you ask of God's spirit, what do you **need** from Him? Speak to God about this.

BROWN-ROA, a division of Harcourt Brace & Company

Reading:

Romans 8:14–17

Meditation:

Some people've never met God
    either in His written word
    or in forgiveness
    or in faith (which is superhuman)
    or in their neighbor (who's altogether too human)
    or in their lives (which are too worldly)
and yet fondly hope to meet Him in heaven.

We have to shatter this expectation, remedy this
    misconception before it leads to utter ruin.

If we haven't found God on earth, we won't find Him in
    heaven.
    For heaven's not some other world where we go to
      escape;
    the kingdom of heaven's already in us, and we have to
    build it up with the graces God gives us.

God wants people who'll work with Him, not sit
    around and dream.
    If we're content to await the kingdom of God, it'll
    never come.
    His gifts in us are living and efficacious;
    they must produce results, and they retain their
      true character as gifts only if we give them to
      someone else in turn.
"This is eternal life:
    knowing You, the only true God,
    and Him whom You've sent—Jesus Christ."

From *That Man Is You* by Louis Evely (Mahwah, NJ:
Paulist Press, 1964).

BROWN-ROA, a division of Harcourt Brace & Company

Gospel:	Luke 4:16–22
Homily:	"Our Church Needs You"
Presenting of Gifts:	Teachers receive religious gift.
Sponsor's Blessing:	(Sponsors face their confirmation candidate, placing their right hand on his/her shoulder).

We have come a long way, you and I . . . and the time for making promises has come.

Tomorrow night, you will stand before the bishop as a follower of Jesus.

I, too, stood before the Church and asked for the gift of the Holy Spirit. I, too, promised to be faithful to Jesus and His Church.

I promise you tonight that I will be your friend, that I will stand behind you, and that I will be your companion as we both grow into persons of God's spirit.

And so I bless you:

May the Lord keep you from all harm and bless you with every good gift.

May He set His word in your heart and fill you with lasting joy.

May you walk in His way, knowing what is right and good.

May almighty God bless you, the Father, Son, and Holy Spirit.

(Trace the sign of the cross on the forehead of the candidate.)

Amen.

BROWN-ROA, a division of Harcourt Brace & Company

Practice for Candidates and Sponsors:

Directions

Closing Song:

Holy God, We Praise Thy Name

Holy God, we praise thy name;
Lord of all, we bow before thee;
All on earth thy scepter claim,
All in heaven above adore thee.
Everlasting is thy reign!

Hark! the loud celestial hymn;
Angel choirs above are raising;
Cherubim and Seraphim,
In unceasing chorus praising,
Fill the heavens with sweet accord:
Holy, Holy, Holy Lord!

BROWN-ROA, a division of Harcourt Brace & Company

Confirmation Liturgy

Theme: Come, Holy Spirit, renew us all, especially those to be confirmed so that they may commit themselves to God.

Entrance Procession: Trumpet and organ

Procession of Bishop and Concelebrants: "Come, Holy Spirit," Choir and congregation (choose a version familiar to parish)

Greeting: **Bishop:** In the name of the Father, and of the Son, and of the Holy Spirit.
Bishop: Peace be with you.

All: And also with you.

Opening Comment: Student

Blessing and sprinkling of holy water

Gloria: Sung

Opening Prayer: Missalette

Liturgy of the Word

First Reading: Isaiah 42:1–5

Responsorial Psalm: Choir and congregation, Psalm 104 (sung): "Lord, send out your spirit and renew the face of the earth."

Second Reading: I Corinthians 12:4–11

Gospel Acclamation: "Come, Holy Spirit" (Choir)

Gospel: (Pastor) John 14:23–26

Liturgy of Confirmation

Presentation of the Candidates: Pastor (The congregation shows its approval of the candidate by applause.)

Homily: Bishop

Renewal of Baptismal Vows: (After the homily, the candidates stand and the bishop questions them. They respond together.)

Renewal of Baptismal Promises:	Missalette
Prayer:	The bishop gives his assent to their profession of faith and proclaims the faith of the Church.
Imposition of Hands:	Kneel. (This is a biblical gesture by which the gift of the Holy Spirit is invoked.)
Prayer of Bishop:	Bishop and priests raise both hands in imposition over all of the candidates.
Anointing with Chrism:	Congregation sits. Bishop anoints his right thumb with chrism and makes sign of the cross on the forehead of the one to be confirmed as he says, "Be sealed with the gift of the Holy Spirit."
General Intercessions:	Students pray their petitions.
Presentation Song:	"Earthen Vessels," John Foley, *Glory & Praise* 1
Prayer over the Gifts:	Bread, water and wine, baptismal candles, and Confirmation journals are brought forward by students.
The Eucharistic Prayer III	
Memorial Acclamation:	Choir and Congregation "Keep in Mind . . ." (Missalette)
Doxology:	Choir and Congregation (Missalette)
Communion Rite	Missalette
The Lord's Prayer:	Recited
Rite of Peace	Missalette
Communion Hymn:	"On Eagles' Wings," Michael Joncas, *Glory & Praise* 2
Communion Meditation:	Students
Prayer after Communion:	Missalette
Concluding Rite	Missalette
Solemn Blessing:	Bishop prays.
Recessional Hymn:	"Yahweh, the Faithful One," Dan Schutte, *Glory & Praise* 1
Recessional:	Trumpet and organ play until all recess.

Confirmation

First Reading:

Isaiah 42:1–3

A reading from the book of the prophet Isaiah.

Here is my servant whom I uphold,
my chosen one with whom I am pleased.
Upon whom I have put my spirit;
he shall bring forth justice to the nations.
Not crying out, not shouting,
not making his voice heard in the street.
A bruised reed he shall not break,
and a smoldering wick he shall not quench. . . .

This is the Word of the Lord.

Response: Thanks be to God.

BROWN-ROA, a division of Harcourt Brace & Company

Confirmation

Second Reading:

1 Corinthians 12:4–11

There are different gifts but the same Spirit; there are different ministries but the same Lord; there are different works but the same God who accomplishes all of them in everyone. To each person the manifestation of the Spirit is given for the common good. To one the Spirit gives wisdom in discourse, to another the power to express knowledge. Through the Spirit one receives faith; by the same Spirit another is given the gift of healing, and still another miraculous powers. Prophecy is given to one; to another power to distinguish one spirit from another. One receives the gift of tongues, another that of interpreting the tongues. But it is one and the same Spirit who produces all these gifts, distributing them to each as he wills.

This is the Word of the Lord.

Response: Thanks be to God.

BROWN-ROA, a division of Harcourt Brace & Company

Confirmation

Gospel:

John 14:23–26

Jesus answered and said to him, "Whoever loves me will keep my word, and my Father will love him, and we will come to him and make our dwelling with him. Whoever does not love me does not keep my words; yet the word you hear is not mine but that of the Father who sent me. I have told you this while I am with you. The Advocate, the holy Spirit that the Father will send in my name—he will teach you everything and remind you of all that I told you.

This is the gospel of the Lord.

Response: Praise to you, Lord Jesus Christ.

BROWN-ROA, a division of Harcourt Brace & Company

Confirmation

General
Intercessions:

First Student:
For Bishop _____ and all our bishops and priests that God will bless their ministry with courage and compassion.

Second Student:
For the Church, that the witness of Christ will strengthen the People of God and challenge us to renewal.

Third Student:
For our parents, sponsors and teachers, that the love and example they have given will be nurtured and cherished throughout our lives.

Fourth Student:
For all of us who are confirmed, that the commitment to witness that we made today will be the focus of our future.

Choir Response

Fifth Student:
For all those suffering in body, mind, or spirit, that the healing power of the Lord will bring them hope, joy, and peace.

Sixth Student:
For all our relatives and friends who have completed their earthly journey, that their inspiration will live on in us.

Choir Response

BROWN-ROA, a division of Harcourt Brace & Company

Confirmation

1. O God of light,
   O Lord of sight,
   You have graces us with Your vision.
   Help us to see Your love everywhere.
   Open our eyes to truth and beauty.
   We love You, Lord,
   For You have saved us.
   Lord, be with us always.
   We are Yours forever.

2. We stand filled again,
   This time with worth.
   We are touched by Your divine presence.
   We are sacred . . . Your spirit lives in us.
   We are healed . . . You are a loving, forgiving Father.
   Amen to the Father, the Son, and the Holy Spirit.

3. **Wisdom:** Enable us to see things as God sees them. Through the guidance of the Holy Spirit, let us see things as Jesus did. Let us witness Jesus' values wherever we go.

4. **Understanding:** Help us to make our own the knowledge of God, His revelation to us, and His working in our human lives. Help us to cherish our faith.

5. **Counsel:** Help us to be receptive to the Holy Spirit and to judge situations according to God's Will. Let us be open to the community support and advice.

6. **Fortitude:** Help us to have courage to trust and rely on God. Help us to overcome our fear of rejection and live out our Christian faith.

7. **Knowledge:** Help us to appreciate created things in relation to God, to value our faith, and to apply it to our daily lives. Holy Spirit, open our minds and hearts to God's Word wherever it is found.

8. **Piety:** Holy Spirit give us piety. Let us approach God as a loving Father and ask what we can do to

BROWN-ROA, a division of Harcourt Brace & Company

show love for God and others. Give us a special love for the Eucharist.

9. **Fear of the Lord:** Let us approach God as a loving Father, yet know God is above us and we stand and kneel in awe at His Presence. As Christians, let us have a healthy fear of any kind of separation from God through selfishness and sin. Help us to work with the Kingdom of God here and now.

BROWN-ROA, a division of Harcourt Brace & Company

Eucharistic Marian Celebration
"To Jesus through Mary"

Altar cloth is designed with children's silhouettes. (See handout.)

Theme: We gather to give praise to Jesus through Mary his Mother.

Entrance Procession: Cross bearer, candle bearer, children carrying posters on Mary's life, Lectionary held high, and priest.

Gathering Song: "Sing of Mary" (Traditional Quaker melody)

Penitential Rite: "Lord have mercy, Christ have mercy, Lord have mercy."

Opening Prayer: Sacramentary

First Reading: Isaiah 7:14
(Student)

Psalm: Psalm 34:1 (Chant)

Second Reading: Luke 1:26–36
(group of children)

Gospel Acclamation: Cantor: Alleluia (three times) sung
All: Alleluia

Cantor: "Blessed are you among all women, Mary, and blessed is the child that you will bear." (see Luke 1:42)

All: Alleluia

Gospel: Luke 1:46–55 (Mary's prayer of praise)

Homily: Mary's role in our lives

General Intercessions: Students

Preparation Hymn: "Hail Mary: Gentle Woman," Carey Landry, *Glory & Praise* 1

Gifts Procession: Two children carry bread and wine.

Holy, Holy, Holy: From *Hi God 2*

Memorial Acclamation: Choir "Christ has died . . ." (Missalette)

The Lord's Prayer	Recited—Join hands.
Lamb of God:	Recite.
Communion Hymn:	"Do You Love Jesus?" Carey Landry, *Hi God!* and "One Bread, One Body" John Foley, *Glory & Praise* 2
Communion Thanksgiving:	Prayer Reflection read by student
Prayer after Communion:	Celebrant
Recessional Song:	"Immaculate Mary" (Missalette)

Eucharistic Marian Celebration

First Reading:
Isaiah 7:14–15

Therefore the Lord himself will give you this sign: the virgin shall be with child, and bear a son, and shall name him Immanuel.

Psalm: 34:1: (chanted by choir)
I will bless the Lord at all times: his praise shall be ever in my mouth.

BROWN-ROA, a division of Harcourt Brace & Company

Eucharistic Marian Celebration

Second Reading:

Luke 1:26–36

This reading lends itself easily to pantomime. You need a reader, the Angel Gabriel (white cassock and tinsel halo), and Mary (white cassock, veil, or blue shawl).

Reader:
In the sixth month, the angel Gabriel was sent from God to a town of Galilee named Nazareth to a virgin betrothed to a man named Joseph, of the house of David. The virgin's name was Mary.

(Mary enters and kneels.)

Reader:
Upon arriving, the angel said to her:

(Angel enters, stretches hands above and over Mary.)

"Rejoice, O highly favored daughter! The Lord is with you. Blessed are you among women."

(Mary bows head and crosses arms.)

Reader:
She was deeply troubled by his words, and wondered what his greeting meant. The angel went on to say to her:

"Do not fear, Mary. You have found favor with God. You shall conceive and bear a son and give him the name Jesus. Great will be his dignity and he will be called Son of the Most High. The Lord God will give him the throne of David his father. He will rule over the house of Jacob forever and his reign will be without end."

(Mary stretches her hands in front of her.)

Reader:
Mary said to the angel, "How can this be since I do not know man?"

(Mary then folds hands in prayer. The angel raises right hand over Mary.)

BROWN-ROA, a division of Harcourt Brace & Company

Reader:
The angel answered her: "The Holy Spirit will come upon you and the power of the Most High will overshadow you; hence, the holy offspring to be born will be called the Son of God."

(Angel Gabriel and Mary exit.)

BROWN-ROA, a division of Harcourt Brace & Company

Eucharistic Marian Celebration

General Intercessions:

Celebrant:
We ask God our Father to help us grow in love for Him and one another, as Mary did. Please respond, "Lord, hear our prayer."

Student:
For our leaders, our pope, and our bishop, that, like Mary, they may be faithful servants of the Lord, let us pray.

All: Lord, hear our prayer.

For all Christians, that, like Mary, they may always keep God's word in their hearts, let us pray.

All: Lord, hear our prayer.

For all those within our parish, that, like Mary, we may help bring one another to Jesus, let us pray.

All: Lord, hear our prayer.

For all those among us who are sick, suffering, or lonely, that they may receive from us the care and the concern that Mary showed for Jesus, let us pray.

All: Lord, hear our prayer.

BROWN-ROA, a division of Harcourt Brace & Company

Eucharistic Marian Celebration

During the week before the celebration, children are given outline silhouettes.

(small, intermediate, larger)

Children color and dress up the silhouettes and put their names on shirt.

Each child cuts out his/her self-portrait. They are collected and checked over for names. Children and assistants (Junior High helpers) pin children's self-portraits on large white material. This material, designed with children's portraits, is draped over the altar.

"Here I am, coming to
Jesus through Mary."

BROWN-ROA, a division of Harcourt Brace & Company

Marian Prayer Service

May Crowning

A Prayer Service in Honor of Mary, the Mother of God.

Graduates:

Processional (Grades K–7 remain seated.)

Opening Song:

Please stand and join us in our opening song, "Immaculate Mary." It is found in the Missalette.

Leader 1:
Introduction:

Mary is our Queen and our Mother.
Mary fully and responsibly accepted the will of God. She heard the Word of God and acted on it. Mary is an example of true charity and service. We gather this day to honor Mary. Mary leads us to Jesus. May we, too, hear God's Word in our lives and act upon God's Word.

Leader 2:

Events in Mary's life are related to our life today. This service calls us to recognize the "hailing" and "blessed" moments that occur in the ordinariness of our daily lives.

Choral Group:
"Hail, Mary, full of grace, the Lord is with you."

Leader 2:

Mary hears this greeting, and she is amazed, surprised, and full of wonder. Her wonder is mixed with doubt and trust, with expectation and readiness. She experiences the hiddeness of God; the mystery of His Presence. "Hail, Mary," the Angel Gabriel said. How incredible is the mystery of God's call!

Blessed in joy and pain . . .

All: Hail, Mary.

Blessed in hope and fear . . .

All: Hail, Mary.

Blessed in light and doubt . . .

All: Hail, Mary.

BROWN-ROA, a division of Harcourt Brace & Company

Blessed in sorrow . . .

All: Hail, Mary.

Blessed in birth and giving birth . . .

All: Hail, Mary.

Blessed in spirit and mother care . . .

All: Hail, Mary, Blessed, Blessed are you, Mary, among all women.

Leader 3:

Mary, remind us that God graces us every time He greets us in our daily tasks, through our relationships with others, and the ordinary happenings of each day.

Help us to let God be God.

Teach us to free our minds of resentment and prejudice, of worldly fears and attachments. Help us to treasure the graced moments coming in a smile . . . a word of comfort . . . a whisper of hope . . . a note of thanks . . . a letter of friendship . . . a touch of affection . . . and the outstretch of care. Help us, Mary, to let God be God.

Show us how to be open to your call, Lord, whether it be in things, events, or persons. Let us take time to review all the times God greeted (hailed) us today.

Please respond, "Yes, Lord!"

All: Yes, Lord.

Moments God called you to be patient . . .

All: Yes, Lord.

Moments God called you to forgive . . .

All: Yes, Lord.

Moments God called you to suffer . . .

All: Yes, Lord.

Moments God called you to act in His name . . .

All: Yes, Lord.

BROWN-ROA, a division of Harcourt Brace & Company

Moments God called you to try another way . . .

All: Yes, Lord.

Moments God called you to recognize His presence . . .

All: Yes, Lord.

Moments God called you to wonder . . .

All: Yes, Lord.

Song:

Immaculate Mary" (verses one and two)

Leader 3:
And the Angel Gabriel said:

Cantor:
Hail Mary, full of grace, the Lord is with you. Blessed are you among women.

Leader 3:
Blessed are you among all women, **Mary.** You stand exquisite . . . holy . . . humble . . . courageous.

Among all women, you are the most happy.

You are the most blessed.

Choral Group:
Hail Mary, full of grace, the Lord is with you. Blessed are you among women and blessed is the fruit of your womb.

Leader 4:
Rejoice, O highly favored daughter! The Lord is with you. Blessed are you among women.

Leader 5:
Mary was deeply troubled by his words, and wondered what his greeting meant. The angel went on to say to her:

BROWN-ROA, a division of Harcourt Brace & Company

Leader 4:

Do not fear, Mary. You have found favor with God. You shall conceive and bear a son and give him the name Jesus. Great will be his dignity, and he will be called the Son of the Most High.

Leader 5:

Mary said to the angel:

Leader 6:

How can this be since I am a virgin?

Leader 5:

The angel answered her:

Leader 4:

The Holy Spirit will come upon you and the power of the Most High will overshadow you; hence, the holy offspring will be called Son of God.

Leader 5:

Mary answered:

Leader 6:

I am the servant of the Lord. Let it be done to me as you say. (See Luke 1:28–38.)

Leader 5.

God's Word takes flesh wherever there is one who says, "Let it be done!" Mary, you teach us to direct our eyes to Jesus whenever we desire to know the Way of the Father.

Choral Group:

Whenever we want faith . . .

All: Mary, help us look to Jesus.

Choral Group:

Whenever we need integrity . . .

All: Mary, guide us to look to Jesus.

Choral Group:

Whenever we need hope . . .

All: Mary, turn us to Jesus.

BROWN-ROA, a division of Harcourt Brace & Company

Choral Group:
Whenever we need life . . .

All: Mary, turn us to Jesus, the everlasting fruit of your womb.

Choral Group:
Hail Mary, full of grace, the Lord is with you. Blessed are you among women, and blessed is the fruit of your womb, Jesus! Holy Mary, Mother of God!

BROWN-ROA, a division of Harcourt Brace & Company

Crowning and Procession

Please stand for the Procession to the statue of the Blessed Mother, and please sit for the Crowning Ceremony. The eighth graders will present their symbolic offerings of candles, symbolic of Mary's Son Jesus, the Light of the World, and flowers, symbolic of Mary, the new Eve and the dawning of new creation.

All pray the Act of Consecration to Mary

All:

Holy Mary, Mother of Jesus,
I entrust myself to your special protection
this day,
every day,
and at the hour of my death.

I consecrate to you my family,
my friends,
my country,
and the whole human race.

Confident that whatever I commend to your care
will be preserved strong and joyful
and will belong most truly to your Son, Jesus Christ.

Reign over us, Mary,
as we pass through joy and sorrow,
through health and sickness.

Help us to follow Jesus faithfully.
Protect us from sin.
Preserve us in good health.
Mother of God, be our Mother.
Watch over the people of God and
lead us to Jesus who died and rose for us.

BROWN-ROA, a division of Harcourt Brace & Company

Priest (Leader): Father God, we thank You for blessing Mary so wonderfully to be the Mother of Your Son. We thank You for giving her to us as our Mother. Help us to follow her example and accept her motherly care. We pray through Jesus Christ our Lord. Amen.

Closing Hymn: "Hail Mary: Gentle Woman," Carey Landry, *Glory & Praise* 1

BROWN-ROA, a division of Harcourt Brace & Company

Ascension Thursday

Theme:	Jesus ascended to His Father. Although we cannot see Him, Jesus promised to be with us always. Jesus invites us to be His witnesses. We gather on Ascension Thursday to celebrate Eucharist.
Entrance Procession:	Traditional
Gathering Song:	"I Have Loved You," Michael Joncas, *Glory & Praise* 2
Penitential Rite:	"Lord have mercy, Christ have mercy, Lord have mercy."
First Reading:	Acts of the Apostles 1:3–11 (Three Junior High Students)
Alleluia:	"Go out to the whole world and preach the good news." Sing Alleluia (Missalette)
Gospel:	Matthew 28:16–20
Homily:	Seven students (grades two–eight) present short witness testimonies.
General Intercessions:	Celebrant prays the petitions.
Preparation Hymn:	"Here I am Lord," Dan Schutte, *Glory & Praise* 3
Gifts Procession:	Two First-Communion children carry bread and wine.
Holy, Holy, Holy:	"Holy, Holy, Holy Lord," Lucien Deiss, *Glory & Praise* 3
Memorial Acclamation:	"When We Eat this Bread," Carey Landry, *Glory & Praise* 1
Amen:	From "Lilies of the Field," *Reader's Digest*
The Lord's Prayer:	Missalette
Sign of Peace:	Handshake
Lamb of God:	(Sung) "Lamb of God," Joe Zsigray, *Glory & Praise* 1
Communion Hymn:	"One Bread, One Body," John Foley, *Glory & Praise* 1 (Bell Choir Chime Group: "Isaiah 49" Carey Landry, *Glory & Praise* 1
Recessional Song:	"City of God," Dan Schutte, *Glory & Praise* 3

Preparation:

Each grade level (two through eight) send representatives to DRE Room and the children write Witness Testimonies answering the following questions:

Tell how we can follow Jesus' way in our own life.
How can you witness through prayer?
How can you witness through work?
How can you witness through play?

Discuss the questions. Talk about witness and bring out ordinary ways we can show forth Christ in our lives.

Encourage the students to be concrete about their practices. Choose one way rather than many.

First . . .

Next . . .

Finally . . .

Review witness talks with students.

Before the celebration of Mass, students prepare readings and talks while using microphone and procedures in coming to altar and place to sit during celebration.

BROWN-ROA, a division of Harcourt Brace & Company

Ascension Thursday

Acts 1:
3–11

First Reader:
In the time after Jesus' suffering he showed them in many convincing ways that he was alive, appearing to them over the course of forty days and speaking to them. . . . He told them not to leave Jerusalem: "Wait, rather, for the fulfillment of my Father's promise, of which you have heard me speak. John baptized with water, but within a few days you will be baptized with the Holy Spirit."

Second Reader:
While they were with him, they asked, "Lord, are you going to restore the rule to Israel now?" His answer was: "The exact time is not yours to know. The Father has reserved that to himself. You will receive power when the Holy Spirit comes down on you; then you are to be my witnesses in Jerusalem, throughout Judea and Samaria, yes, even to the ends of the earth." No sooner had he said this than he was lifted up before their eyes in a cloud which took him from their sight.

Third Reader:
They were still gazing up into the heavens when two men dressed in white stood beside them. "Men of Galilee," they said, "why do you stand here looking up at the skies? This Jesus who has been taken from you will return just as you saw him go up into the heavens."

This is the Word of the Lord.

Response: Thanks be to God.

BROWN-ROA, a division of Harcourt Brace & Company

Ascension Thursday

General Intercessions:

Please respond, "Bless us and make us one."

Celebrant:
That all nations under God be united in peace, we pray.

Response: Bless us and make us one.

Celebrant:
That all leaders, the pope, bishops, priests, and religious, and leaders of all countries be united in Christian love and care, we pray.

Response: Bless us and make us one.

Celebrant:
That all of us present follow the ways of Jesus, our Brother. May we be true witnesses and prepare our hearts for the gift of the Spirit, we pray.

Response: Bless us and make us one.

Celebrant:
Heavenly Father, we ask all these petitions in the name of the Father, and of the Son, and of the Holy Spirit.

Response: Amen.

BROWN-ROA, a division of Harcourt Brace & Company

Graduation Mass

Theme: Graduation is a time to celebrate the love of our God and our call to radiate love in our daily lives. We, as a community, gather to praise and remember in this Eucharistic celebration.

Introductory Rite

Entrance Song: "Glory and Praise to Our God," Dan Schutte, *Glory & Praise* 1

Greeting: Celebrant

Graduation Welcome: Principal or teacher

Penitential Rite: Missalette

Glory to God: Choice of liturgy planners

Opening Prayer: Celebrant

Liturgy of the Word

First Reading: Proverbs 4:1–7

Responsorial Psalm: "Isaiah 49," Carey Landry, *Glory & Praise* 1 (Bell Chime Choir: optional)

Second Reading: Jeremiah 1:4–10

Gospel: Matthew 5:14–16

General Intercessions: Students

Liturgy of the Eucharist

Gift Procession: Students bring gifts and symbols while commentator explains offering.

Preparation Hymn: "All I Ask of You," Gregory Norbet, OSB, *Glory & Praise* 3, or *Listen* (Weston)

Invitation to Pray and Prayer over Gifts: Celebrant

Memorial Acclamation: "Dying He destroyed our death, rising He restored our life, Lord Jesus come in glory."

The Lord's Prayer	Recited
Rite of Peace	
Peace Song:	"Song of Thanksgiving," Joe Zsigray, *Glory & Praise* 2
Lamb of God:	Recite
Communion Hymn:	"On Eagles' Wings," Michael Joncas, *Glory & Praise* 2, "Earthen Vessels," John Foley, *Glory & Praise* 1
Recessional Hymn:	"All My Days," Dan Schutte, *Glory & Praise* 1

Graduation Mass

Liturgy of the Word

First Reading:
Proverbs 4:1–7

Hear, O children, a father's instruction, be attentive, that you may gain understanding! Yes, excellent advice I give you; my teaching do not forsake. When I was my father's child, frail, yet the darling of my mother, he taught me and said to me: "Let your heart hold fast my words: keep my commands, that you may live!"

"Get wisdom, get understanding! Do not forget or turn aside from the words I utter. Forsake her not, and she will preserve you; love her and she will safeguard you. The beginning of wisdom is: get wisdom; at the cost of all you have, get understanding."

This is the Word of the Lord.

Response: Thanks be to God.

Second Reading:
Jeremiah 1:4–10

The word of the Lord came to me thus: Before I formed you in the womb I knew you, before you were born I dedicated you, a prophet to the nations I appointed you. "Ah, Lord God!" I said, "I know not how to speak; I am too young . . ."

But the Lord answered me, say not, "I am too young." To whomever I send you, you shall go; whatever I command you, you shall speak. Have no fear before them, because I am with you to deliver you, says the Lord. Then the Lord extended his hand and touched my mouth, saying, "See, I place my words in your mouth! This day I set you over nations and over kingdoms: To root up and to tear down, to destroy and demolish, to build and to plant."

BROWN-ROA, a division of Harcourt Brace & Company

Graduation Mass

General Intercessions:

After each petition please respond, "Lord, hear our prayer."

First Student:
For the Class of _____, that we will continue to share our talents and abilities for the good of others and the Church, we pray to the Lord.

Response: Lord, hear our prayer.

Second Student:
For our Holy Mother the Church, her bishops, priests, religious, and laity, that the Lord continue to build and strengthen the People of God, especially here at _____, we pray to the Lord.

Response: Lord, hear our prayer.

Third Student:
For our parents, families, and friends, all those special people we carry in our hearts, that God will reward them for all the love and encouragement they have shown us, let us pray to the Lord.

Response: Lord, hear our prayer.

Fourth Student:
For all those who find it difficult to celebrate, that they are able to rediscover the hope of the Resurrection, let us pray to the Lord.

Response: Lord, hear our prayer.

Fifth Student:
For all those who are sick or confined, that the healing presence of God will bring them joy and peace, let us pray to the Lord.

Response: Lord, hear our prayer.

Sixth Student:
For peace and justice, that we may actively participate in bringing unity and harmony to our world, let us pray to the Lord.

BROWN-ROA, a division of Harcourt Brace & Company

Response: Lord, hear our prayer.

Seventh Student:
For our friendships, that they may be as long lasting and as true as God's love for us, let us pray to the Lord.

Response: Lord, hear our prayer.

Eighth Student:
For all our friends and relatives who are deceased, that they may eternally enjoy God's peace and love, let us pray to the Lord.

Response: Lord, hear our prayer.

Ninth Student:
For the Class of _____, that the Holy Spirit will guide and protect us and give us the courage to say no when the world wants to hear yes.

Response: Lord, hear our prayer.

Priest:
Heavenly Father, hear our prayers and bless all here present, especially the Class of _____. We ask this in the name of Your Son, Jesus, through the Holy Spirit.

Response: Amen.

BROWN-ROA, a division of Harcourt Brace & Company

Closing School Liturgy

Theme:	We come together in thanksgiving for our priests and teachers, for our classmates, and for the closing of the year. We look forward to a very happy vacation.
Entrance Procession:	Cross bearer, servers, representative from each class carrying a class collage or banner, Eucharistic ministers, lector carrying book high, and priest celebrant form the procession.
Gathering Song:	"Sing a New Song," Dan Schutte, *Glory & Praise* 1
First Reading:	1 Corinthians 1:3–9
Responsorial Psalm:	"I Have Loved You," Michael Joncas, *Glory & Praise* 2 (Sing the refrain twice.)
Second Reading:	1 Thessalonians 5:18
Gospel Acclamation:	"Alleluia," Erich Sylvester, *Glory & Praise* 1
Gospel:	Mark 5:18–20
General Intercessions:	Students, first through eighth grades
Preparation Hymn:	"Yes, Lord, Yes," Carey Landry, *Hi God 2*
Gifts Procession:	Two children carry bread and wine.
Holy, Holy, Holy:	Missalette (Choose one familiar to parish.)
Memorial Acclamation:	"Christ has Died . . ." *Glory & Praise* 1
Amen:	"Amen," Erich Sylvester, *Glory & Praise* 1
The Lord's Prayer:	Recite
Lamb of God:	Recite
Communion Hymn:	"God Is So Good," Carey Landry, *Glory & Praise* 3
Communal Thanksgiving:	Students
Recessional Hymn:	"Though the Mountains May Fall," Dan Schutte, *Glory & Praise* 1

Closing School Liturgy

A reading from the first letter of Paul to the Corinthians.

Grace and peace from God our Father and the Lord Jesus Christ.

I continually thank my God for you because of the favor he has bestowed on you in Christ Jesus, in whom you have been richly endowed with every gift of speech and knowledge. Likewise, the witness I bore to Christ has been so confirmed among you that you lack no spiritual gift as you wait for the revelation of our Lord Jesus Christ. He will strengthen you to the end, so that you will be blameless on the day of our Lord Jesus (Christ). God is faithful, and it was he who called you to fellowship with his Son, Jesus Christ our Lord.

This is the Word of the Lord.

Response: Thanks be to God.

BROWN-ROA, a division of Harcourt Brace & Company

Closing School Liturgy

Second Reading:
1 Thessalonians 5:18

. . . For all things give thanks to God, because this is what he expects you to do in Christ Jesus.

We praise You, God; we acknowledge You as Lord; Your Church praises You around the world.

BROWN-ROA, a division of Harcourt Brace & Company

Closing School Liturgy

General Intercessions:

Please respond, "Lord, hear our prayer."

First Student:
For our priests who gave of themselves so generously to our school family this year, let us pray to the Lord.

Second Student:
For our teachers who help us to grow and develop as true followers of Jesus, let us pray to the Lord.

Third Student:
For our classmates who worked, played, and prayed with us during the past year, let us pray to the Lord.

Fourth Student:
For our parents who love and support us on the way, let us pray to the Lord.

Fifth Student:
For the poor and those who need friendship and love, let us pray to the Lord.

Sixth Student:
For the sick and disabled, let us pray to the Lord.

Seventh Student:
For peace and justice in our world, let us pray to the Lord.

Eighth Student:
For our graduates, that God direct them along the future and keep them safe in God's care, let us pray to the Lord.

Priest:
Heavenly Father, bless all of us and give us a safe and happy summer.

Hear our prayers through Jesus Christ our Lord.

Response: Amen.

BROWN-ROA, a division of Harcourt Brace & Company

Closing School Liturgy

Thanksgiving Psalm:

Psalm 100

First Student:
Sing joyfully to the Lord, all you lands;
serve the Lord with gladness;
come before him with joyful song.

Second student:
Know that the Lord is God;
he made us, his we are;
his people, the flock he tends.

Third student:
Enter his gates with thanksgiving,
his courts with praise;
Give thanks to him; bless his name,
for he is good:
the Lord, whose kindness endures
forever,
and his faithfulness, to all generations.

Fourth student:
Thank God for His goodness in giving us Jesus.
May each of us be blessed during our summer vacation
and may we remember to praise the Lord in worship.

BROWN-ROA, a division of Harcourt Brace & Company

Ribbon Ceremony for Graduates

1. Graduates process in.

2. Opening Comment—Student.

3. Each grade states a wish for the graduates.

4. Ribbons are blessed.

5. Ribbons distributed by principal and pastor; names to be called by teachers.

6. Readings by eighth graders.

7. Girl's choir sings.

8. Graduates process out.

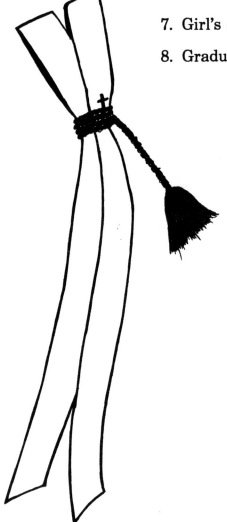

This prayer celebration was written by Jeanine McCarten. Used with permission of the author.

BROWN-ROA, a division of Harcourt Brace & Company

Ribbon Ceremony

Ribbon 1:

Today ribbons mean:

We've made it! We're graduating!

They stream downward and we look at them proudly as a badge won after eight years of hard work.

They are a recognition from our school, from our principal and our teachers, our paster and our priests—that today is our day to be honored.

Ribbons are a sign and symbol of celebration.

BROWN-ROA, a division of Harcourt Brace & Company

Ribbon Ceremony

Ribbon 2:

These ribbons are a sign of binding of ourselves to our school and of ourselves to one another—

for part of ourselves will always remain behind

as an investment,

as a legacy,

as a building up of _____ School.

BROWN-ROA, a division of Harcourt Brace & Company

Ribbon Ceremony

Ribbon 3:

Part of ourselves is given in gift to you, our younger classmates, who will follow in our footsteps,

for you who next year and the years after that will tramp the junior high staircase and dream your dreams through the same windows

that have known our hopes and dreams and those of hundreds of ribbon-bearers before us.

BROWN-ROA, a division of Harcourt Brace & Company

Ribbon Ceremony

Ribbon 4:

Ribbons have a rich history.

They mark in some way all of the important moments in our lives.

In birth, that most basic ribbon of all is the umbilical cord,

the binding of our newborn self with our mother who transmitted to us the stuff of life itself.

The streamers on our baptismal outfit, like the priestly stole, are an initiation into the life and priesthood of Jesus.

The ribbons are swaddling clothes or receiving blankets, keeping us warm and secure.

Ribbons on birthday presents and gifts for special days.

Ribbons in a school girl's hair.

BROWN-ROA, a division of Harcourt Brace & Company

Ribbon Ceremony

Ribbon 5:

Streamers on our bikes as we begin to venture out into the big wide world.

Ribbons on a kite string.

Ribbons on a winning science project or book report or art work.

Ribbons for winning a swim meet or race.

Ribbons in a book remembering our place for us.

Yellow ribbons tied around trees say, "We remember."

Banners are ribbons written large.

Flags are like ribbons.

We assign to their colors and designs a sense of country and countrymen.

BROWN-ROA, a division of Harcourt Brace & Company

Ribbon Ceremony

Ribbon 6:

In the years ahead we will discover other kinds of ribbons.

Ribbons on prom flowers.

Ribbons on wedding flowers.

Ribbons on the Christening dress of our own yet-to-be-born children.

BROWN-ROA, a division of Harcourt Brace & Company

Ribbon Ceremony

Ribbon 7:

Ribbons worn as arm bands in a march or for a cause.

Ribbons to be cut in ceremony for a new beginning.

Olympic ribbons.

Ribbons on a soldier's chest.

A handkerchief waving goodbye becomes a white ribbon just like the white flag of surrender or peace.

And at the very end of life are the ribbons of purple and black that hang as buntings over an entry way, signs of mourning and respect for someone who has died.

Ribbons of a winding-shroud like the ribbons Jesus accepted as His friends wrapped His broken body for the tomb.

BROWN-ROA, a division of Harcourt Brace & Company

Ribbon Ceremony

Ribbon 8:

Ribbons are for binding.

Ribbons bind us to one another.

Ribbons are for waving.

Let us celebrate these ribbons as ties of blue and white

that bind us to _____ School,

to each other, and to You.

BROWN-ROA, a division of Harcourt Brace & Company

Ribbon Ceremony

To conclude our Ribbon Ceremony today, we ask that
_____ step forward as a representative of
the Class of _____ to accept this candle as a symbol
            year
of loyalty and dedication to the traditions of _____.
                                         school
May this candle light the way as you travel on your journey . . .

As St. Luke reminds us:

"No one lights a lamp and puts it under a bushel basket
or under a bed; he puts it on a lampstand so that
whoever comes in can see it. There is nothing hidden
that will not be exposed, nothing concealed that will not
be known and brought to light. Take heed, therefore, how
you hear: to the man who has not, will lose even the little he thinks he has."

Luke 8:16–18

BROWN-ROA, a division of Harcourt Brace & Company

Music Resources

Focus on Music. Dubuque, IA: BROWN Publishing-ROA Media, 1986.

Glory & Praise, Volume 1. Phoenix, AZ: North American Liturgy Resources, 1979.

Glory & Praise, Volume 2. Phoenix, AZ: North American Liturgy Resources, 1981.

Glory & Praise, Volume 3. Phoenix, AZ: North American Liturgy Resources, 1983.

Landry, Carey. *Hi God!* Phoenix, AZ: North American Liturgy Resources, 1975.

Landry, Carey. *Hi God 2.* Phoenix, AZ: North American Liturgy Resources, 1975.

Reader's Digest Family Songbook of Faith and Joy. Pleasantville, NY: Reader's Digest Association, 1978.

Seasonal Missalette. Chicago, IL: J.S. Paluch Company.

We Celebrate: Companion Hymnal to We Celebrate Seasonal Missalette. Chicago, IL: J.S. Paluch Co., yearly.

Young People's Glory & Praise. Phoenix, AZ: North American Liturgy Resources, 1985.

BROWN-ROA, a division of Harcourt Brace & Company